Thomas Henry Edsall

History of the Town of Kings Bridge

Now Part of the 24th Ward, New York City

Thomas Henry Edsall

History of the Town of Kings Bridge
Now Part of the 24th Ward, New York City

ISBN/EAN: 9783337415365

Printed in Europe, USA, Canada, Australia, Japan

Cover: Foto ©ninafisch / pixelio.de

More available books at **www.hansebooks.com**

HISTORY

OF THE

TOWN OF KINGS BRIDGE

NOW PART OF THE 24TH WARD
NEW YORK CITY

WITH MAP AND INDEX

BY

THOMAS H. EDSALL
MEMBER OF THE N. Y. HISTORICAL SOCIETY

NEW YORK CITY
PRIVATELY PRINTED
1887

ing mainly of micaceous gneiss or granite,[1] the former largely preponderating, the exposed surfaces indicating subjection to intense heat and pressure, with so great displacement that the strata are nearly vertical, outcropping in numerous parallel ledges, not continuous, but *en echelon*, and giving steep inclination to hillsides. A coarse, crystallized limestone[2] of varying hardness, ranging about north-northeast, crops out at King's Bridge and on the Whiting and Delafield estates, Spuyten Duyvil Ridge. On the latter ridge the surface of the primary rocks is strewn with trap boulders.

DISCOVERY.—The earliest known visitor to this locality was Henry Hudson. Going up the river which bears his name, he skirted its westerly shore September 13, 1609, and, on his return, was attacked, October 2d, from *Shorack-Kappock*, the Indian name of Spuyten Duyvil Point,[3] and the kill or creek at its base.

INDIANS.—The Indian name of this section was *Weckquaeskeck*,—"the birch-bark country,"—and its residents were known to the first settlers as *Wickers-*

---

[1] Affording building-stone of fine quality. Before 1750 quarries of "broken stone" were worked on Spuyten Duyvil Ridge, the whole extent of which is scarred by them. The large quarries at Spuyten Duyvil Point were worked until about 1850.

[2] Known as *King's Bridge Marble*. It was extensively quarried early in the century on the northerly end of Manhattan Island. Perkins Nicholls had a marble-sawing mill at "Dyckman's Cut" (which was excavated to supply power to this mill by the ebb and flow of the tide), and another at the King's Bridge. On the banks of the Hudson, along the base of Spuyten Duyvil Ridge, were several kilns for making lime from this stone, all of which have been disused for many years.

[3] According to tradition, the natives had a castle or stronghold on the point.

creek Indians. In person they were tolerably stout. Their hair was worn shorn to a coxcomb on top, with a long lock depending on one side. They wore beaver and other skins, with the fur inside in winter and outside in summer, and also coats of turkey feathers. They were valiant warriors. "Yea," says De Vries, "they say they are *Manetto*—the devil himself!" Their leading sachems, at the advent of white settlers, were *Tequemet, Rechyawac* and *Packamiens*, from whom the Dutch director, Kieft, purchased, in August, 1639, the tract *Keskeskick*. This tribe gradually dwindled, until its remnant finally disappeared before the end of the eighteenth century.

FIRST SETTLEMENT.—The earliest white resident and proprietor was Dr. Adraien Van der Donck, *juris utriusque doctor*, of Leyden. He had been sheriff of the Colonie of Rensselaerswyck since 1641. Having aided Director Kieft in negotiating an important Indian treaty at Fort Orange, Albany, the latter granted him, in 1645, a large tract on the Nepperhaem River, Yonkers, where he built a saw-mill,[1] laid out farms and plantations and "had actually resolved to continue." But that indispensable requisite of a Dutch farm, salt meadow, was lacking. In search of this, Van der Donck found, about a mile above the *wading-place* (King's Bridge) "a flat, with some convenient meadows about it," which he promptly secured by purchase from the Indians and a further grant from Kieft. His new acquisition included the area under consideration, extending from

---

[1] Hence the name of "Saw Kill," by which this stream became known.

the Hudson to the Bronx, and from the Spuyten Duyvil Creek to the Nepperhaem tract. Here he located his *bowerie*, or home-farm, with its "planting-field," and near the latter he had already begun the erection of his house, before going to Holland, in 1649, as the representative of the commonalty of New Amsterdam. Van der Donck's "planting-field" was on the plain or flat of the Van Cortlandt estate, lying between Broadway and the present lake, and extending up to the southerly end of Vault Hill.[1] It is probable that his house was on the flat, and located, perhaps, where the old house of Jacobus Van Cortlandt afterwards stood until the early part of this century.[2]

While absent in Holland, Van der Donck's lands were erected into the fief or Colonie of Nepperhaem (or, as he called it after his own name, *Colendonck*), and he was made its patroon. Pursuant to the "Freedoms and Exemptions," he sent out to it, from Holland, a number of colonists with supplies of farming stock and implements. In 1652 he was about to return to his colonie, and had already embarked his wife, mother, brother and sister, with an ample stock of goods, when the West India Company prevented his departure.[3] During his detention he got

---

[1] It may have also stretched eastward across the brook and beyond the site of the present lake.

[2] Its site was just behind the present grove of locusts, north of the Van Cortlandt Mills.

[3] Van der Donck had so well accomplished his mission on behalf of the oppressed commonalty as to procure from the States General their mandate, recalling Stuyvesant to Holland, of which he was made the bearer. But the States being on the eve of war with England, and needing the assistance of the rich and powerful West India Company, the latter was enabled to not only procure the revocation of Stuyvesant's recall, but to detain its bearer in Holland.

word that some "land-greedy" persons were squatting on his lands. He appealed to the company to protect his possession of the "flat and meadows;" also for leave to return to them, which was withheld until 1653. In the summer of that year he sailed for Nieuw Netherland, arriving in the autumn, and repaired to his *bowerie*. He did not long survive his return, dying in 1654 or 1655. The latter was the year of the Indian massacre, when all the surviving settlers about Nieuw Amsterdam fled to the fort for protection. It is probable that Van der Donck's bowerie was deserted and destroyed. In August, Stuyvesant granted to a Cornelis Van der Donck a parcel of about fifty morgens, on the north side of Manhattan Island, "by the savages called *Muscoote*, or a flat (*anders een vlacte*)," and as much meadow or hay land as was given to other boweries. This may have referred to the late Dr. Van der Donck's bowerie, but no further mention has been found of the grantee or his connection with this tract.

After the patroon's death his widow joined her father, the Rev. Francis Doughty, in "the Virginias," where she became the wife of Hugh O'Neale, of Patuxent, Maryland.

The province had passed under English rule, and nearly ten years had elapsed since the death of her first husband before Mrs. O'Neale took any steps to reclaim the Yonkers estate. On the 21st of September, 1666, she and O'Neale went before Governor Nicoll and his Council, accompanied by several Indians, who had formerly owned the lands. The latter made acknowledgment of their sales to the late patroon,[1] and on the 8th of October a grant of the whole estate was made to O'Neale and wife. On the 30th they assigned their patent to Elias Doughty, of Flushing, L. I., a brother of Mrs. O'Neale, probably for convenience of sale, on account of their residing at a distance.

The first to purchase from Doughty was John Archer, or *Jan Arcer*, as he signed his name. He was the son of Jan Aarsen, from Nieuwhoff, who was nick named by the Dutch *Koop-al* (buy-all), and the son was known as Jan Koop-al, the younger. He had long resided at Oost Dorp (now Westchester). In March and September, 1667, he bought about one hundred and twenty acres of upland and thirty acres of meadow, near the "wading-place." On the upland, just across the meadow from Paparinamin, he founded the village of Fordham. It had the countenance and protection of the Governor, being " in a " convenient place for the relief of strangers, it being " the road for passengers to go to and fro the maine, " as well as for mutual intercourse with the neighbor- " ing colony." The village consisted of about a dozen houses in an extended line, along the base of Tetard's Hill, crossed at the middle by the "old Westchester path" (Albany post road), leading up over the hill towards Connecticut. No traces of these old habitations remain. Two years later Archer acquired all

---

[1] Of "a certain parcel of land upon the maine, not farre from West- " chester, commonly called ye Yonnekers Land." They declared its bounds to be " from a place called *Macackesin* at ye north, so to come to *Nepera* " and to ye Kill *Sorquapp*, then to *Muskota* and *Papperenemen* to ye south " and crosse ye countrey to ye eastward of Bronckx his River and " Land."

the land southerly to High Bridge, lying between the Harlem and Bronx, which was erected into his Manor of Fordham in 1671. The north line of this ancient manor from the Harlem to the Bronx, being the south line of the O'Neale patent,[1] became one of the southerly boundaries of the town of King's Bridge. Archer lived and ruled at Fordham in frequent contention with his tenants and neighbors until his death, in 1684. During the Dutch re-occupation, in 1673–74, his government was suspended, and the inhabitants of Fordham nominated their own magistrates; but on the return of the English, in the latter year, Archer resumed his sway. In 1679 he was sheriff of New York. At his death the manor was so heavily mortgaged to the wealthy Dutchman, Cornelis Steenwyck, that his heirs could not redeem it. By Steenwyck's will it was devised to the "Nether Dutch Reformed Congregation," in New York, for the support of their minister.

---

[1] Notwithstanding the patent for the Manor of Fordham recited that it was part of the land " granted in the Grand Patent to Hugh O'Nea'e & Mary, his wife ;" also that " purchase was made thereof by John Archer from Elyas Doughty, who was invested in their interest, *as also of the Indyan Proprietors*, &c.," it is impossible, by any interpretation of the boundaries in the O'Neale Patent to make them extend below the north line of the manor. There is no *record* of any deed from Doughty to Archer of land south of that line. The writer is of opinion that Archer, conniving with the Governor or Secretary Nicoll, advanced this claim of title through Van der Donck's successors, in order to forestall claims to the tract which might have been otherwise established. Such claims were preferred early in the following century by Quimby against the Dutch Church, which then owned it, and about 1750 a brief on behalf of the church in an ejectment suit sets out with a recital of a *copy* of an *unrecorded* deed from Doughty to Archer, on which, however, counsel was not instructed to rely. The only proper basis of Archer's title was his purchase from the "Indyan Proprietors."

William Betts and George Tippett, his son-in-law, next purchased from Doughty (deed, July 6, 1668), about two thousand acres, extending across from the Hudson to the Bronx, south of an east and west line which went along the north side of "Van der Donck's planting-field." This line struck the Hudson about three hundred feet south of Thorn's dock, and the Bronx about five hundred feet south of the Yonkers city line, and the purchase included all south of it, excepting Paparinamin, for which Tippett received a separate "deed of gift" from Doughty. It included "that piece where formerly the old Van der Donck's house stood," and what are now Spuyten Duyvil, Hudson Park, Mosholu, Van Cortlandt's, Olaff Park, Woodlawn Heights and Woodlawn Cemetery. Betts and Tippett obtained from Governor Lovelace, February 20, 1671, a patent which contained a proviso that it should no way prejudice "the New towne of ffordham," nor what had been done by his order towards its settlement.

Mr. Betts was an Englishman, and by trade a turner. He was at Scituate, Mass., in 1635, four years after which he married Alice, a "maiden of the Bay," who bore him several children. With his minister, Lothrop, he removed to Barnstable, and thence came to Connecticut. In 1662 he lived at Oost Dorp, where he was a magistrate by appointment of Stuyvesant. He was named as a patentee in the English patent for the town of Westchester, granted in 1668. The same year he removed to his new plantation in the Yonkers, and the next year became overseer of the court at Fordham. He died in 1675, survived by his wife, Alice, sons, Samuel, Hopestill and John, a daughter, Mehitable, wife of George Tippett, and a grandson, John Barrett, son of a deceased daughter, Hannah, who had married Samuel Barrett, of Westchester. Descendants of the name of Betts continued to own portions of the ancestral acres until the early part of this century.

Mr. Tippett was at Flushing in August, 1667, when he gave in his name to the Governor "to be ready to serve his Majesty" on all occasions. While he lived in the Yonkers the swine of the New Harlem people used to run at large at the upper end of Manhattan Island, and sometimes straying across the *wading-place* at low tide, failed to return. Tippett would be charged with their detention and the whole community hauled into court as witnesses. Tippett's "ear-mark" for his own swine was said to be "the cutting of their ears so close that any other marks might be cut off by it." Mr. Tippett died intestate in 1675, survived by his wife, Mehitable (afterward married to Lewis Vitrey and Samuel Hitchcock), a son George, perhaps a son Henry, and a daughter Mehitable (who was married first to Joseph Hadley and second to John Concklin). Descendants of his name held portions of the estate until the Revolutionary War.

"Tippett's Hill" was the name of Spuyten Duyvil Neck during the same period,[1] and the principal stream of the Yonkers has always been called after him, although corrupted into "Tibbits" in recent times.

---

[1] Known after the Revolution and until recent'y as "Berrien's Neck," after an owner who married Dorcas Tippett, a great-great-granddaughter of the first George.

John Hadden [1] made the next purchase from
Doughty. His deed of June 7, 1668, antedates that
of Betts and Tippett, but bounds on land already
sold to them. It conveys three parcels aggregating
three hundred and twenty acres, lying directly north
of Van der Donck's planting-field and extending
across from the Albany post road to the road to Mile
Square. The Van Cortlandt estate now includes the
whole of it. For two hundred acres Hadden gave a
horse and for the remainder five pounds! In December, 1668, Betts sold to Hadden twenty-four acres
adjoining his "house in the old field."

Mr. Hadden was a carpenter by trade. He settled
in the Yonkers with his sons-in-law, George Clevinger and William Smith, and in 1672 he was made overseer of the village of Fordham. His sons-in-law dying a few years later, Mr. Hadden sold out and returned to Westchester, where he and his descendants
were respected citizens.

Doughty next sold the remainder of the O'Neale
patent (excepting "Mile Square," already disposed
of) to Thomas Delavall, Fredryk Flypsen and Thomas
Lewis.[2] It was conveyed to them November 9, 1672,
by purchase from Delavall, and the heirs of Lewis Flypsen subsequently acquired their interests. The tract

---

[1] In early records and MSS this name is sometimes written "Heddy," "Hedger," etc.

[2] This was probably the sale for which Mrs. O'Neale "received a good part of her payment in horses and mares," with which she was about to "return home into Maryland, ye place of her abode;" but hearing report of a prohibition against importing horses to that colony, she procured a letter to its Governor from Governor Lovelace, of New York, asking a dispensation from the rigor of the late order in her case so as to permit her to dispose of her horses in Maryland to her best advantage

contained about eight thousand acres. Riverdale, Mount St. Vincent and a part of Woodlawn Heights are located on the southerly part of this purchase.
Mr. Flypsen was a carpenter by trade. He came to Nieuw Amsterdam in Stuyvesant's time, under an engagement with the West India Company for five years, during which time he worked on the forts at Nieuw Amsterdam and Esopus. He married, in 1662, Margaret Hardenbrook, widow of Peter Rudolphus de Vries, a successful trader. Margaret was also engaged in trade, which she continued after this marriage, going to and from Holland as supercargo of her own vessels, in one of which, the "Charles," she brought over the Labadists, in 1679. By her "fortune, thrift and enterprise" and his exertions, Mr. Flypsen became the richest man in the colony. After the death of Margaret he married, in 1692, Catherine Van Cortlandt, widow of John Dervall and daughter of Olaf Stevenszen Van Cortlandt, by whom he received further additions to his wealth. Mr. Flypsen purchased other large tracts of land in Westchester County. In 1693 he procured the erection of the whole into the Manor of Phillipsburgh, in which the "island Paparinamin" was included. The old *manor-house* is now the city hall in Yonkers. For twenty years Mr. Flypsen was a member of the Council. He died in 1702, aged seventy-six, survived by a son Adolphus, a daughter Annetje, wife of Philip French, an adopted daughter Eva, wife of Jacobus Van Cortlandt, and a grandson Frederick (son of his deceased son Frederick,) to whom he devised the Yonkers plantation.

THE FERRY.—Soon after the village of Fordham

was settled the people of New Harlem tried to divert eastern travel from the *wading-place* to the new ferry they had set up between New Harlem and Bronx-land. They obstructed the banks at Spuyten Duyvil[1] with fences, but travelers threw them down and still crossed at the ancient ford without paying toll. In the summer of 1669 the ferry was removed to Spuyten Duyvil, " a nearer and more convenient passage to and from the island and the Maine," and Johannes Verveelen was made ferryman. There was allotted to his use the "island or neck of land Paparinamin." where he was required to provide a dwelling-house furnished with three or four good beds for the entertainment of strangers; also provisions at all seasons for them, their horses and cattle, with stabling and stalling; also a sufficient and able boat to transport passengers, horses and cattle on all occasions.[2] A causeway was also

---

[1] This curious appellation, whose origin has never been satisfactorily explained, seems to have been applied to a strip of shore on the Manhattan Island side of the wading-place, then to the crossing itself and the creek leading therefrom to the Hudson, and finally to the neck which still retains it. It means "spouting devil," and may have arisen from some peculiar *upburst* of water as the tide rushed over the reef which obstructs the channel at that point. Mr. Riker has ingeniously suggested the outpour from the guns of the " Half-Moon ;" also the gushing spring under Cock Hill; but the explanation in Irving's quaint and humorous legend of the ' Trumpeter' will ever meet with popular acceptance.

[2] " YE FERRYMAN—HIS RATES.

" For lodging any person, 8 pence per night, in case they have a bed with sheets ; and without sheets, 2 pence in silver.

" For transportation of any person, 1 penny silver.

" For transportation of a man and horse, 7 pence in silver.

" For a single horse, 6 pence.

" For a turn with his boat, for 2 horses, 10 pence ; and for any more 4 pence apiece ; and if they be driven over, half as much.

" For single cattle, as much as a horse.

required to be built across the meadow from Paparinamin to Fordham, of which Verveelen was to bear one-third of the expense and Fordham the remainder. Archer called on Betts, Tippett and Hadden to help him build his share of the "*causey.*" They demurred, being more interested in having a bridge made over the Bronx to East Chester. The dispute came before the Governor, who decided that Betts, Tippett and Hadden should first aid with the causeway,[1] and then the Fordham people should help them build the bridge. For so doing the ferry was made free to Betts, Tippett and Hadden. Verveelen kept the ferry many years and was succeeded by his son Daniel, who was ferryman until the erection of the King's Bridge.

During the last quarter of the seventeenth century the Betts, Tippett and Hadden families, and those who had intermarried with them, and their retainers and servants composed all the population of the Yonkers outside of Fordham and Paparinamin. Their homes were grouped about a mile north of Fordham, where they had a "good and strong block-house."[2] During King Philip's War, in 1775, there were fears of an Indian outbreak in this colony. Archer summoned Betts, Tippett and Hadden to aid him in the fortification and defense of Fordham. They remonstrated

---

"For a boat loading of cattle, as he hath for horses.

"For droves of cattle to be driven over, and opening ye gates, 2 pence p. piece.

"For feeding of cattle, 3 pence in silver.

"For feeding a horse one day or night with hay or grasse, 6 pence."

[1] This causeway was on the line of the present McComb Street.

[2] They probably stood in the neighborhood of the present Van Cortlandt mansion.

before Governor Andros that they should not "bee bound to leave their houses and goods and to please the humours of the said Mr. Archer, thereby perhaps to lose all what they have." The Governor excused them from work on the defenses of Fordham, but he warned them to "be vigilant at their own place and keep watch upon all occasions."

THE KING'S BRIDGE.—The increasing travel between New York and "the Maine" demanded a bridge in place of the ferry. As early as 1680 the Council of Governor Andros had ordered "Spiting Devil" to be viewed with reference to a bridge there. A bill to erect one was introduced in the Assembly in 1691. The next year Governor Fletcher recommended its construction by the city of New York, but the municipal authorities were deterred from the undertaking by the "great expense." In January, 1693, Fredryck Flypsen offered to build one at his own expense, if he could have certain "easy and reasonable toles."[1] In June the franchise was granted to Mr. Flypsen for ninety-nine years. The bridge was to be twenty-four feet wide, and to be free for all the King's forces, and was to be named the "King's Bridge." It was built during the year, a few rods east of the present one.[2] It had a draw for the passage of such craft as navigated the Harlem and a gate, set up at the end, where

---

[1] To wit: "1 penny for each head of neat cattell; 2 pens for each mann and horse, and 12 pens for each score of hoggs and sheep that shall pass the said brige; and 9 pens for every boat, vessell or cannoo that shall pass the said brige, and cause the same to be drawne up."

[2] The removal to its present site was made pursuant to an act of Assembly passed in 1713 at the petition of Flypsen's grandson, Frederick Phillipse, then a minor.

KING'S BRIDGE.

the keeper received the tolls.[1] A public-house was kept open at the north side for the "entertainment of strangers." The bridge was owned by Mr. Flypsen's grandson and great-grandson, in succession, until it was forfeited by the latter, Colonel Frederick Phillipse, because of his adhesion to the crown in the war of independence.

During the first half of the eighteenth century the Yonkers was sparsely peopled. Jacobus Van Cortlandt bought a plot of fifty acres, known as "George's Point,"[2] from Mr. Flypsen, in 1699, and added to it several hundred acres while he lived, forming the bulk of the present Van Cortlandt estate. He made a mill-pond by damming up the Tippett's Brook, and set up a grist and saw-mill. In 1704 there were about twenty families in the Yonkers. The Betts and Tippett families partitioned their tract in 1717, and gradually sold it off to new settlers. Agriculture was the chief industry, and the farms were noted for choice fruits and fine breeds of cattle. Produce was carried to market in periaugers. Stone quarrying was engaged in before the middle of the century.

The main highways were the Albany and Boston post roads—the former opened to the Saw-kill about 1669, and the latter opened on the line of the Old Westchester Path to East Chester about 1671. The travel by land was almost wholly on horseback. The

---

[1] Madame Knight, crossing December, 1704, enroute to Boston, was charged three pence "for passing over with a horse."

[2] So called after George Tippett (2d), who conveyed it in 1691, to his brother-in-law, Joseph Hadley. He sold to Matthias Buckout, who conveyed to Mr. Flypsen.

common roads were very poor. The mail to
Albany was carried by foot-post. That to Boston was
taken by post-riders once in three weeks, which time
was shortened in 1731 to once a fortnight. The stage-
coach to Boston began running in 1772.

THE FREE BRIDGE.—The King's Bridge was unpop-
ular because of its tolls; also its barrier gate, which made
the belated traveler furious as he shouted to awaken
the drowsy gate-keeper several rods away. A popular
subscription was started in 1756 for building a free
bridge. Benjamin Palmer[1] headed the movement,
and when enough was subscribed, he attempted to
build it where the first bridge had stood. Colonel
Phillipse, who owned the shore on Paparinamin,
naturally objected. Palmer had to go farther down
the Harlem. He interested with him Jacob Dyckman, on the island, and Thomas Vermilye, on the
Westchester side, and they began the work from land
of the former to that of the latter. Colonel Phillipse,
"because he knew it would stop his bridge from taking tolls," tried to prevent its construction. Twice in
one year he caused Palmer's impressment "as a
soldier to go to Canada," which compelled him to
employ and pay for substitutes. But in spite of oppo-
sition the structure was completed at the close of
1758. It was opened with a grand barbecue on New
Year's Day, 1759, and hundreds of people attended
from New York City and Westchester County, and
"rejoiced greatly."[2] A new road was built to connect

---

[1] Who attempted to found a city as a rival to New York, on an island
in the Sound, since called "City Island."

[2] Dyckman, who built a tavern at the approach to the free bridge
(where the King's Bridge Hotel now stands), failed soon afterward, and

the bridge with the Albany and Boston roads, and for a time all travel ceased across the King's Bridge. Colonel Phillipse's bridge-keeper finding his occupation gone, threw up his lease, and the proprietor had to advertise for a new tenant. It is probable that attempts to collect tolls were abandoned soon afterwards.

In 1763 the Rev. John Peter Tetard purchased from Petrus Vermilye a farm of sixty acres, near King's Bridge, lying on the old Boston road, to which he removed about three years later. In 1772 he opened there a French boarding-school, probably the first in New York, where, besides French, he taught "the most useful sciences, such as geography, the doctrine of the spheres, ancient and modern history, etc." The house was destroyed during the Revolution. The old stone archway yet standing near its site is variously called "Dominie Tetard's Wine Cellar," the old "powder magazine," the "old bakery," etc., but its real purpose is unknown.[1]

---

sought legislative relief for his outlays in its construction. Palmer, towards the end of the century, unsuccessfully applied to the Assembly for aid on the same account. The press took up his cause and declared that his work had been "the first step towards freedom in this State, * * * "for it was almost as difficult for Mr. Palmer to get a free bridge in "those days as it was for America to get her freedom." Aaron Burr and others made up a purse of £30 for the needy old man in 1800.

[1] Dominie Tetard was born in Switzerland about 1721; graduated from University of Lausanne and received ordination about 1752; soon after was pastor of French Church, Charleston, S. C.; came to New York 1756; married Frances, daughter of Robert Ellison; became assistant pastor of Church du St. Esprit, taking charge 1764–66, until a new minister could be engaged in Europe. After his removal to King's Bridge he used to preach in Fordham Dutch Church. He was commissioned July 6, 1775, French interpreter to General Schuyler and chaplain to the troops in

Across the Boston road from Tetard's farm was one of about seventy-five acres, which Richard Montgomery purchased and occupied in 1772, pursuant to his long-cherished wish to leave the service and engage in husbandry.[1] His house stood on the brow of the hill, near the Boston road,[2] and there he lived until his marriage to Janet Livingston and removal to another farm he had purchased near Rhinebeck.[3] The King's Bridge farm was devised to his sister Sarah, Viscountess Ranelagh, by the will found by Arnold among his papers at Quebec, a few days after his untimely death. Fort Independence was erected on this farm, a few hundred yards north of the house which, with the out-buildings, orchards, fences, etc., was completely destroyed during the Revolution.

THE REVOLUTION.—The inhabitants of the Yonkers were generally opposed to all efforts of the British ministry to establish arbitrary government in the colonies. Colonel Phillipse sided with the crown and tried to control his tenants. At their head, he was present at the meeting held at the White Plains, April 11, 1775, to appoint deputies to a convention; but he declined "to have anything to do with

---

the Colonie," with pay of major, and went with General Montgomery to Canada. He served as chaplain during the war, and on the reorganization of Columbia College, in 1784, was made professor of French, and so continued until his death, December 6, 1787, in his sixty-sixth year.

[1] So declared in a letter shortly prior to his resignation. He meant to come to America, "where his pride and poverty would be much more at their ease."

[2] A little way inside of the gateway of Mr. William Ogden Giles.

[3] *New York Gazetteer*, October 7, 1773, contains his advertisement of the King's Bridge farm "at private sale."

deputies or congresses." After protesting against "such illegal and unconstitutional proceedings," he led off his followers. Colonel James Van Cortlandt and his brother Frederick, of the Yonkers, heartily favored resistance.

The news from Lexington was shouted at every threshold along the old Boston road in the night of April 22d, as the herald spurred on towards New York. A few days later the inhabitants were aiding to unload, at King's Bridge and the hills beyond, upward of one hundred cannon,[1] which had been carted out from the city for security. On the 8th of May the new committee for Westchester County, on which Frederick Van Cortlandt represented the Yonkers, chose Colonel James Van Cortlandt as deputy to the new Provincial Congress, and he attended its first meeting at the exchange in Broad Street.

The importance of maintaining communication by land between New York and the country so impressed the Continental Congress that it resolved, on May 25th, that a post should be immediately taken and fortified at King's Bridge. On the 30th the Provincial Congress appointed a committee of five, including Captain Richard Montgomery and Colonel James Van Cortlandt to view the ground near the bridge and report whether it would admit of a tenable fortification. Their report of June 3d favored a post for three hundred men on the hill adjoining Hyatt's tavern, but recommended no form or dimensions and thought it imprudent to fortify until the embodi-

---

[1] Compensation to the heirs of Sebring and Beekman, for certain of these guns, was provided for by an act of the Legislature, passed in 1800.

ment of troops, who could do most of the labor. Commanding points on Tippett's and Tetard's Hills were suggested for additional works. On the spots thus indicated forts were afterwards erected by the Americans, and when captured by the British, were strengthened and garrisoned by them for many years.[1]

Colonel Van Cortlandt was a member of the committee of the Provincial Congress to arrange the troops and form the militia. Frederick Van Cortlandt, Thomas Emmons, Williams Betts and William Hadley were of the local committee for the Yonkers. Under their supervision a militia company was formed in the precinct, as part of the "South Battalion" of the county. The roster included sixty-four names,—Anthony Allaire, Abraham Asten, George Berrien, Wm. Betts, Frederick, Gilbert and Robert Brown, Hendrick Browne.Jr., Henry Bursen, Jno. Cock, Jno. and Edw'd Cortright, Geo. and Jas. Crawford, Jno. Cregier, Daniel Deen, John Devoe, Abraham Emmons, Benj., Thos. and Robert Farrington, Usial Fountain, Wm. and Isaac Green, Geo., Isaac, Jos. and Wm. Hadley, Thos. Merrill, Jas. Munro, Jos. Jr., and Thos. Oakley, Abraham and John Odell, Jas. Parker, Abm. Dennis, Isaac, Israel, Jacob, Lewis, Martin and Wm. Post, Henry Presher, Tobias Rickman, Wm. Rose, Edward and John Ryer, Francis Smith, Chas. Elnathan, Jr., Elijah, Henry and Jacob Taylor, Izarell Underhill, Frederick Van Cortlandt, Abm, Frederick and Josh. Vermilye, John and Wm. Warner,

[1] The British called the redoubt on the hill near Hyatt's tavern "*Ft. Prince Charles;*" the one on Tippett's Hill "*Number Three*, and the one on Tetard's Hill, the American Ft. Independence, "*Number Four.*"

Geo. Wertz, John and Samuel Williams. On August 24, 1775, they chose John Cock, captain; Wm. Betts, first lieutenant; John Warner, second lieutenant; and Jacob Post, ensign. The names were sent to the Provincial Congress for commissions. The county committee protested against the captain elect, and on the 11th of September presented the affidavit of William Hadley, of the district committee, that when he presented the "general association" to Cock, he said, "I sign this with my hand, but not with my heart; for I would not have signed it, had it not been for my wife and family's sake." The friends of Cock rallied to his support. A majority of the company and a score more inhabitants of Yonkers [1] sent down a petition in his favor, stating that he had been chosen "for his well-known skill and ability in the military discipline," and that the complaints were made out of "spite and malice." But further affidavits by Isaac Green and George Hadley, that Cock "had damned the Continental Congress," satisfied the Committee of Safety that it was improper to give Cock a commission. The local committee was ordered to hold a new election, "taking care to give public notice that John Cock cannot be admitted to any office whatsoever." [2]

---

[1] They were Matthias, Anthony and Benjamin Archer, Benjamin Arsdan, Stephen Bastine, Ezekial and Henry Brown, George Crawford, Benjamin Farrington, Jonathan Fowler, John Guerenean, Samuel Lawrence, Henry and Jordan Norris, David, Jr., and Moses Oakley, Abm., James and Thomas Rich, Elnathan Taylor and Thomas Tippett.

[2] Cock kept the old tavern on the north side of King's Bridge. The head of the overthrown statue of George III., in the Bowling Green, was carried to Fort Washington, to be fixed to a spike on the flag-staff. While it was left temporarily at Jacob Moore's tavern, near by, an emissary

The twenty-one nine-pounders carried off from the Battery by the Sons of Liberty, August 23d, were hauled up to King's Bridge and left with the rest in care of the minute men. In the night of January 17, 1776, more than fifty guns near Williams', and as many in the fields near Isaac Valentine's, were spiked or "loaded and stopped with stones and other rubbish." Search was made for the perpetrators. John Fowler was brought before the Committee of Safety on the 23d, charged with a recent purchase of rat-tail files in New York. He implicated William Lounsbery, of Mamaroneck, as the real purchaser. They were imprisoned. Jacamiah Allen was employed to un-pike the guns at twenty shillings each. He raised them on fires of several cords of wood, tended day and night to soften the spikes, and by March 16th he had unspiked eighty-two and expected to soon complete the work. These guns were afterwards mounted in the works erected by the American troops on the hills about King's Bridge.

In February, 1776, Augustus Van Cortlandt, clerk of New York City, reported to the Committee of Safety that for their security he had removed the public records to Yonkers. They were deposited in Colonel Van Cortlandt's family burial vault[1] and

from Colonel Montresor went out through the "rebel camp" with a message to Cock to steal and bury the head. This was done probably at Cock's tavern), and when the British arrived, in November, 1776, it was dug up and sent in care of Lady Gage to Lord Townsend, "to convince them at home of the infamous disposition of the ungrateful people of this distracted country."

[1] This ancient depository of the city records is still used as a burial-place by the family, and gives the name to the hill on which it is located.

were still there in December; but it is probable the British were soon afterwards apprised of their place of concealment and had them returned to the city.

On the 18th of March the Yonkers militia held a new election and chose John Warner, captain; Jacob Post, first lieutenant; Samuel Lawrence, second lieutenant; and Isaac Post, ensign. In May the Provincial Congress had in service the armed schooner "General Putnam," commanded by Captain Thomas Cregier, of King's Bridge. After months of inactivity at the heads of inlets when he should have been at sea, Cregier was discharged for inefficiency and the vessel was sold.

Early in June Washington visited and inspected the grounds above King's Bridge. He found them to admit of seven places well calculated for defense. "Esteeming it a pass of the utmost importance in order to keep open communication with the country," he set two Pennsylvania regiments at work on their fortification, and put bodies of militia to the same labor as fast as they arrived. In General Orders of July 2d, Mifflin was directed to repair to King's Bridge and to use his utmost endeavors to forward the works. "*The time is now at hand which must probably determine whether Americans are to be freemen or slaves*" is a memorable sentence in this order. The enemy was ready to disembark in the lower bay. It was unknown from what quarter their attack would come. Mifflin thought they would divert attention to the heights above King's Bridge, and it was reported they meant to erect strong works there to cut off communication between city and country. On the 12th of July the ships of war "Rose" and "Phœnix" sailed up the Hudson, and unaware of the new batteries which had been planted on Tippett's and Cock Hills, anchored near the mouth of Spuyten Duyvil Creek. A dozen guns opened fire on them and "did great execution." On the 15th additional troops were hurried out to King's Bridge, the destruction of which was apprehended. Three hundred men were sent up the Harlem River in boats on the 19th and were put to work on the forts. Engineers were assigned, tools supplied and the work carried on night and day during the ensuing fortnight. On the 8th of August General Clinton was directed to send expresses to Ulster, Dutchess, Orange and Westchester Counties, to hasten levies and march them down to the fort erected on the north side of the bridge. On the 13th General Heath was put in command of the division stationed there and large quantities of provisions and ammunition were sent up. The "Rose" and "Phœnix" with their tenders were anchored off Mt. St. Vincent. On the nights of the 14th, 15th and 16th numbers of officers and men, (including on two occasions Generals Heath and Clinton) gathered on Tippett's Hill to witness an attempt to destroy these vessels with fire-ships. It was made at midnight on the 17th. A flaming galley set fire to one of the tenders and consumed her with "horrid flames." At sunrise on the 18th the frigates and remaining tenders fled down stream, and ran through the *chevaux-de-frise* under a heavy cannonade from the "Blue Bell Fort"[1] and Fort Lee. On th 21st Washington assigned the new engineer

---

[1] Fort Washington, near which the old Blue Bell tavern stood.

Monsieur Martin to the post at King's Bridge and under his direction work was pressed on the fortifications. On the 23d Clinton's brigade was ordered into camp. Colonel Thomas's regiment pitched on the south side of Fort Independence, Colonel Graham's about half a mile farther southward, Colonel Paulding's and Colonel Nicholas' on the flat below, near Corsa's orchard, and Colonel Swartwout on the southerly end of Tippett's Hill. On the 25th a detachment went down from King's Bridge to Paulus Hook in "the flat-bottomed boat" and brought back a number of gun-carriages, on which cannon were mounted in the new works. Colonel Swartwout's regiment threw up a battery "on the north side of Spuyten Duyvil Creek, at its very mouth," to prevent the enemy from approaching the bridge in boats, and also constructed two additional redoubts on the top of Tippett's Hill, one of which was called "Fort Swartwout."[1] No "fatigue rum" was allowed to any one engaged on these works, except on certificate that he had been "faithful, obedient and industrious." On the 27th the Provincial Congress, then sitting at Harlem, alarmed by the defeat on Long Island, ordered its records and papers, and the receiver-general's chest to be taken at once to the camp at King's Bridge. On the 29th Heath impressed every boat and craft at the post and hurried them down to Washington for use in the retreat from Long Island. On the 31st the inhabitants began driving their cattle into the interior. The Committee of

---

[1] The night guard in this work, October 17, 1776, was one captain, two lieutenants and fifty men.

Safety now urged on Washington the defensibility of the country above the bridge and the dreadful consequences of its occupation by the enemy. He replied that the defensible state of that ground had not escaped him, and that as the posts at King's Bridge were of such great importance, he hoped the convention would afford aid for their defense. When it became evident in September that the city was untenable by the Americans in the face of the superior British force, Washington determined to take post at King's Bridge and along the Westchester shore, where barracks could be procured for the part of the army without tents. He concluded to leave five thousand men on the island for defense of the city, and to post nine thousand at King's Bridge and its dependencies. On the 8th Heath was instructed to fell trees across the roads towards the bridge, to dig holes in them, break them up and destroy them so as to be impassable. The next day one hundred and sixty thousand boards were ordered for the barracks at the bridge, also brick and stones for ovens, which all soldiers who were masons were ordered to assist in making.

Meanwhile the inhabitants suffered from the occupation of their farms. Fences were pulled down and burned and corn-fields, gardens and orchards pillaged. The orders of the day pronounced it "cruel as well as unjust and scandalous thus to destroy the inhabitants by destroying the little property for which they have been sweating and toiling through the summer and were expecting very soon to reap the fruits of."

Howe's movement to Throg's Neck caused Washington to call a meeting of general officers at King's

Bridge. It was held on the 16th of October, when it was determined to abandon Manhattan Island. On the 19th strong pickets were established and frequent night patrols made through all the region about King's Bridge. On the 20th Washington moved his headquarters to the bridge, where the main army was now in barracks, and continued there until the 22d. During the next few days the army moved off to the heights of the Bronx, leaving garrisons in the forts about King's Bridge under orders to destroy them on the enemy's approach in force. Col. Lasher, in Fort Independence, was "to burn the barracks, quit the post and join the army, by way of the North River, at White Plains." At three in the morning of the 28th the long lines of barracks were fired and the forts abandoned. Their garrisons either withdrew to Fort Washington, or, crossing to New Jersey, rejoined their regiments at White Plains by way of King's Ferry. Gen. Greene, coming out from Fort Washington, found several hundred stand of small arms, great numbers of spears, shot, shells, etc. To carry these off he impressed all the wagons in the neighborhood. He then dismantled King's Bridge and the Free Bridge. On the evening of the 29th General Knyphausen, with a force of Hessians and Waldeckers which had landed at New Rochelle, approached Fort Independence by the old Boston road, and, finding it deserted, occupied it the following day. He took possession of the other works on Tetard's Hill and occupied them until November 2d. Then, with part of his forces, he descended and took a position on Paparinamin, north of King's Bridge. Having repaired the bridge, he crossed over and occupied the deserted American post on the opposite hill, but retired on the 4th. He crossed again on the 7th with fifteen hundred men and took positions on the hills commanding the old King's Bridge road. On the 16th the remainder of General Knyphausen's force crossed over the Free Bridge and united in the capture of Fort Washington, which thereafter took his name.

Being now possessed of the whole of Manhattan Island, the British adopted and strengthened the American works at and about King's Bridge for the defense of New York City. Beginning with the westerly redoubt on Spuyten Duyvil Neck, and going eastward, and from Fort Independence southward, they were distinguished by the numbers 1 to 8, inclusive.

Number One was located where the house of the late Peter O. Strang stands, in grading for which all traces of the fort were obliterated. It was square, and overlooked the Hudson and Spuyten Duyvil Creek at their confluence.

Number Two was a circular redoubt on the crown of the hill in the field west of Warren B. Sage's residence. Its walls are yet discernible.[1] This was the American Fort Swartwout. In the adjoining field to the westward a flanking redan may yet be seen overlooking the Riverdale road.

---

[1] Miscalled "Ft. Independence," on Sauthier's and other British maps, an error which has misled some modern writers. The same misnomer has been perpetuated otherwise. The Coast Survey so calls it in a diagram of the triangulation point on its wall. These errors probably arose from confounding the name "Tetard's Hill," on which Fort Independence stood, with "Tippett's Hill," whereon the fort in question was located.

Number Three stood where Warren B. Sage's house now stands, on the easterly brow of Spuyten Duyvil Hill and directly overlooking the post on the northerly end of Manhattan Island at King's Bridge, called Fort Prince Charles[1] by the British. Numbers one, two and three were first garrisoned in 1777. In November, 1778, the three works had a garrison of one hundred and ten officers and men. They were abandoned by the British in the fall of 1779.

The creek near Johnson's foundry was crossed by a pontoon bridge, and a military road ran from it up the easterly side of the hill to and along Spring Street, where it branched off to the Redoubts One, Two and Three.

Number Four was the American Fort Independence, on Tetard's Hill, across the valley. The house of William Ogden Giles now stands on its site. It was built on the farm of General Richard Montgomery, and may have been laid out by him. It occupied a most commanding position overlooking the Albany road on one side and the Boston road on the other. It had two bastions at the westerly angles.

The British garrisoned it continuously from its capture until they removed its guns, August 16th, its wood-work, August 17th, and demolished its magazine, September 12, 1779. It was not garrisoned again during the war. A number of iron six-pounders were dug up inside its walls, by Mr. Giles, when excavating his cellar, about thirty years ago. Two of them are now mounted in a miniature fort on his grounds.

Number Five was a square redoubt, whose walls are

---

[1] This work is yet standing.

yet standing on the old Tetard farm, a little way north from H. B. Claflin's stables. It is about seventy feet square. It was occupied in 1777, and dismantled September 18, 1779.

Number Six stood just west of the present road to High Bridge, and its site is now occupied by a house formerly owned by John B. Haskin.

Number Seven was on the Cammann place. No trace remains.

Number Eight was on land now owned by H. W. T. Mali and Gustav Schwab. The latter's house occupies part of its site.

King's Battery is on the grounds of Nathaniel P. Bailey, and is still preserved.

Another redoubt, semicircular in form, is yet standing on the old Bussing farm, just north of the town line, and distant about one thousand feet northeasterly from the William's Bridge Station on the Harlem Railroad. It commanded the road and bridge across the Bronx, and was one of the series of works thrown up by Washington along the heights of the Bronx and extending northerly to White Plains, at the approach of Howe. General Heath located it and Colonels Ely and Douglas were engaged upon it October 6, 1776.[1]

An outpost of light troops was established near Mosholu and maintained throughout each year. The force was usually composed of German mounted and

---

[1] Between this fort and Fort Independence, on the southerly side of the Boston road, and on the Corsa farm, stood "Negro Fort," so called, it is said, because garrisoned by a company of negroes from Virginia. The British kept an outguard there in the winter of 1776–77. No trace of it remains, a house now occupying its site.

foot yagers and a company of chasseurs formed of detachments from the different Hessian regiments in New York.[1] Their camp was on Frederick Van Cortlandt's farm, near his house.[2] They made frequent patrols out Mile Square road, over Valentine's Hill and Boar Hill to Phillipse's Mills and back by the Albany post road. Two three-pound *Amusettes* were sometimes taken on these rounds.

Another camp of light troops and cavalry was established at the foot of Tetard's Hill, between King's Bridge and the Free Bridge. It was long occupied by Emmerick's chasseurs, formed in 1777, Simcoe's rangers and other Royalist troops. The King's Bridge was made the *Barrier*, and the old tavern on the north side became the *watch-house*.

During the protracted struggle the Yonkers was the scene of constant military activity. Numerous unsuccessful attempts were made by the Americans to recapture the posts on Tippett's and Tetard's Hills, and plans of winter attacks across the frozen Harlem and Spuyten Duyvil were often laid and foiled. The rangers of Simcoe and De Lancey, the yagers of

---

[1] In 1778 five companies of foot and one of mounted yagers, under Lieutenant Colonel Von Wurmb. In 1779 the yagers and Lord Rawdon's corps.

Captain von Hanger's company of chasseurs, in 1778, consisted of four officers, twelve sub-officers, three drummers and one hundred privates-selected from the Leib, Erb Prinz, Prinz Carl, Donop, Mirback, Trimbach, Losberg, Knyphausen, Woelwarth, Wiessenbach and Sietz Regiments.

[2] Known as the "Upper Cortlandts," in distinction from Colonel Jacobus Van Cortlandt's house on the plain, called "Lower Cortlandts." The former was also called "Cortlandt's white-house" sometimes. It was burned about 1826, and the present residence of Waldo Hutchins was erected on its site.

Von Wurmb and the chasseurs of Emmerick were often met and engaged by troops of American Light Horse, under the fiery Colonel Armand and other dashing leaders, on the high-roads and by-ways of the Yonkers plantation. It was also the scene of ceaseless ravages by those irregular bands, known as "Cowboys" and "Skinners." Most of the inhabitants went into exile, and were refugees within either the American or British lines. Their homes were desolated, their buildings, fences and orchards destroyed. The Tippetts were mainly Tories. In 1776, General George Clinton arrested Gilbert Tippett for "practices and declarations inimical to American liberty." Colonel James De Lancey had married a cousin, Martha Tippett. The Warners, Hadleys, Valentines, Bettses, Corsas, Posts and other old residents were nearly all stanch Whigs, and supplied some of the ablest guides and minute-men of the Revolution.

THE SIEGE OF FORT INDEPENDENCE.—In January, 1777, General Heath made a movement against the British outposts at King's Bridge.[1] His forces were chiefly Connecticut volunteers and Dutchess County militia. They moved down on the night of the 17th, in three divisions—the right, under General Lincoln, from Tarrytown by the old Albany road, to the heights above Colonel Van Cortlandt's; the centre, under General Scott, from below White Plains to the rear of Valentine's house,[2] on the Boston road; and

---

[1] The following account of the movement is condensed from Heath's and contemporary British reports.

[2] Now and for nearly a century past the Varian homestead, an ancient stone house on the northerly side of the road.

the left, under Generals Wooster and Parsons, from New Rochelle and East Chester to Williams' on the east side of the Bronx above the bridge. The three divisions arrived simultaneously at the enemy's outposts just before sunrise on the 18th. General Lincoln surprised the guard above Van Cortlandt's, capturing arms, equipage, etc. Heath moving with the centre, as it approached Valentine's house, ordered its cannonade by Captain Bryant in case of resistance from the guard quartered there, and sent two hundred and fifty men at double-quick to the right into the hollow between the house and Fort Independence to cut off the guard. Just then two British light horsemen, reconnoitering out the Boston road, came unexpectedly on the head of Wooster's column where the road descends to Williams' bridge. Before they could turn, a field-piece dismounted one, who was taken prisoner, while the other galloped back crying "The rebels! the rebels!" which set all outguards and pickets running to the fort, leaving arms, blankets, provisions, tools, etc., behind. Those fleeing from Valentine's and the Negro Fort were fired on and one captured. The American left and centre were then moved into the hollow between Valentine's and Fort Independence, and the surrender of the latter was demanded and refused. The garrison consisted of a body of Hessians and Colonel Rogers' rangers. Heath sent a detachment with two field-pieces southward to the brow of the hill overlooking the Free Bridge,[1] and opened fire on a battalion of Hessians drawn up across the Harlem, back

---

[1] Probably to a point on the old Tetard farm, now Claflin's land.

of Hyatt's tavern. The enemy settled down as the shot passed them, and one piece being moved lower down, they retired rapidly behind their redoubt,[1] receiving a shot as they were turning the point. The enemy now opened on Heath's artillerymen from guns he had not suspected to be in the redoubt, and the men hastily drew their pieces back, receiving several shots before they reached the top of the hill.

The success of this movement on the British outposts flew through the country and was magnified into the reduction and capture of Fort Independence and its garrison. Washington communicated this report to Congress before receiving official accounts, causing a double disappointment when the facts were known. The Tory press in New York City reported it as an attack on Fort Independence by a large body of rebels, who were "bravely repulsed."

On the 19th the enemy opened fire from the fort and killed one American. Heath determined to cut off the British battalion at Hyatt's by passing one thousand men over Spuyten Duyvil Creek on the ice. It was very cold. The men were detached and gathered at Spuyten Duyvil Ridge for the attack, but before morning the weather had so moderated that it was deemed too hazardous to make the attempt. There was cannonading on both sides on the 20th, and the enemy on the island were thrown into much confusion. Heath observing that the enemy, when fired at across the Harlem, found shelter behind the hill at Hyatt's, had a field-piece hauled up to the

[1] The fort on the hill at northerly end of Manhattan Island, overlooking the King's and Free Bridges,—originally built by Americans and called by the British "Fort Prince Charles."

brow of Tippett's Hill, and opened fire on both their front and rear on the afternoon of the 21st. Some of the enemy found shelter in their redoubt, others under the banks; some lay flat on the ground and some betook themselves to the cellars, so that presently there was no object for the gunners. A smart skirmish occurred at Fort Independence on the 22d. To keep up the appearance of serious designs upon the fort, Heath ordered fascines, etc., to be made, and sent for a brass twenty-four pounder and a howitzer from New Castle. Another skirmish took place near the south side of the fort on the 23d, just before dusk, in which the Americans had an ensign and private killed, and five men wounded. On the 24th a severe storm began; Lincoln's division had to quit their huts in the woods back of Colonel Van Cortlandt's, and move back, some even to Dobbs Ferry, to find shelter. A freshet in the Bronx caused the water to run over Williams' bridge. Early on the 25th, the enemy sallied from Fort Independence towards De Lancey's Mills, surprised and routed the guard, wounding several and causing a regiment to quit its quarters. By British accounts they also took one piece of cannon. About ten o'clock they made a sally out the Boston road in force, drove the guards from Negro Fort and Valentine's house, and pushed on so impetuously, keeping up a brisk fire, that the retreating guards threw themselves into the old American redoubt [1] overlooking Williams' bridge. The enemy thereupon lined a strong stone wall a few

---

[1] This old Revolutionary work may still be traced on the hill northwest from the bridge. It is semicircular in form and was laid out by Heath in the fall of 1776.

rods distant to the southwest. Two regiments of militia were at once formed in the road near Williams' house, across the Bronx, and were sent by General Heath, in support of Captain Bryant with his piece, across the submerged bridge. When nearly up the hill on the Boston road, Bryant unlimbered to prevent his horses being shot, and the men took the drag-ropes; but the steepness of the ascent required the dragging of the piece almost within pistol-shot before it could be depressed enough to bear on the enemy. Its first shot opened a breach in the wall four or five feet wide, the next made another opening, whereupon the enemy fled back to Fort Independence with the greatest precipitation. The Americans had two killed and a number wounded. On the 27th the brass twenty-four pounder and the howitzer arrived and opened on the fort. The former sprung her carriage after the third discharge. There were no live shells for the howitzer. No regular cannonade of the fort was, in fact, ever contemplated. Attempts were made to draw the enemy out of the fort. A detachment was sent to Morrisania to light numerous fires at night; and, to induce the enemy to suppose the Americans were collecting there with designs of crossing to New York at or near Harlem, large boats were brought forward on carriages. The British garrison on Montressor's (Randall's) Island, alarmed at this, set fire to the buildings and fled to New York.[1] A brigade of the enemy moved up to

---

[1] By Tory accounts the "rebels" went over to Montressor's Island and "burnt Colonel Montressor's house to the ground, and ravaged whatever they could meet with" on this occasion.

Fort Washington and a detachment was sent for from Rhode Island.

On the 29th a severe snow-storm came on. Gens. Lincoln, Wooster, Scott and Tenbroeck were unanimous that the troops ought to move back where they could be protected from the inclement weather, especially as they had no artillery with which to take the fort, and were opposed to any idea of assault or storm with militia. Accordingly, after dusk, the American forces retired northward and eastward in good order to their former stations, and the siege of Fort Independence was abandoned. The boldness of these operations, by raw militia, and for so long a period, in face of the strong force of British and German veterans in New York, speak volumes for the spirit of our grandsires in their determined contest for independence.

THE MASSACRE OF THE STOCKBRIDGE INDIANS.—During the summer of 1778 the British light troops, which were encamped about King's Bridge, had frequent skirmishes with the American light troops on the highways and by-roads of the old Yonkers.

On the 20th of August, when patrolling out the old "Mile Square Road," Lieutenant-Colonel Emmerick was attacked and compelled to return to his camp at King's Bridge. A few days later a small body of American light troops and Indians, under Colonel Gist, which had taken part in this encounter, was posted in several detachments on the heights commanding the old road, one body on each side of the road, just north of its crossing over a small stream beyond the present Woodlawn Heights, and a third about three hundred yards west of the road, on Devoe's farm, opposite to Woodlawn Heights. Between the last party and the road were scattered about sixty Stockbridge Indians, under their chief, Ninham, who had been in England. Lieutenant-colonel Simcoe, of the Queen's Rangers, learned, through his spies, that the Indians were highly elated at Emmerick's retreat and supposed that they had driven the whole force of light troops at King's Bridge. He took measures to increase this belief and meantime planned to ambuscade and capture their whole force. His idea was, as the enemy came down the "Mile Square Road," to advance past his flanks. This movement would be perfectly concealed by the fall of the ground to the right (*i.e.*, down the slope in Woodlawn Heights, towards the stream at Second Street) and by the woods on the left (*i.e.*, Van Cortlandt's woods, bordering the road and "Lover's Lane," extending north from the road opposite Fourth Street).

On the morning of August 31st the Queen's Rangers, under Simcoe, the chasseurs, under Emmerick and De Lancey's Second Battalion and the Legion Dragoons, under Lieutenant-colonel Tarleton, marched out the "Mile Square Road," reaching the present Woodlawn Heights about ten o'clock. The rangers and dragoons were posted on the right (east of Second Street and about opposite to First Avenue). Emmerick's instructions were to take a position on the left, in Van Cortlandt's woods, near *Frederick* Devoe's house, half a mile up the lane. By mistake he took post in the woods near *Daniel* Devoe's house, which stood on the "Mile Square Road," near the entrance to the lane, and sent a patrol forward on the road. Before Simcoe, who was half-way up a tree reconnoitering, could stop this movement, he saw a flanking party of Americans approach and heard a smart firing by the Indians who had lined the fences alongside the road on Emmerick's left.

The rangers under Simcoe moved rapidly up the stream to gain the heights (Husted's), which were occupied by the Americans under Gist and Stewart, and the cavalry under Tarleton advanced directly up the hill to where Emmerick was engaged (between Third and Fourth Avenues). Being unable to pass the fences bordering the road, Tarleton made a circuit to return on the right (coming to the road again about Fifth Avenue). Simcoe, hearing of Tarleton's difficulty, left the remainder of his corps under Major Ross, and breaking from the rangers with the grenadier company, arrived unperceived (about opposite the end of Sixth Avenue) close upon the left flank of the Indians, who were intent upon the attack of Emmerick and Tarleton. With a yell the Indians fired on the grenadier company, wounding Simcoe and four of his men; but being outnumbered and flanked, the Indians were driven from the fences into the open fields of Daniel Devoe, north of the road. Tarleton and Emmerick then got among them with the cavalry. The Indians fought most gallantly, pulling several of the cavalry from their horses; but overpowered by the superior force of the enemy, they had to flee. They were swiftly pursued up over the fields, across the lane, down through Van Cortlandt's woods, over Tippett's Brook into the woods on the ridge beyond, where a few survivors found concealment among the rocks and bushes, and thus escaped. Nearly forty were killed or desperately wounded, including the old chief Ninham and his son. The former called out to his people to fly, "that he was old and would die there." He wounded Simcoe and was killed by Wright, his orderly hussar. Tarleton had a narrow escape in the pursuit down the ridge. In striking at an Indian he lost his balance and fell from his horse, but luckily for him the Indian had no bayonet and had discharged his musket. During the pursuit Simcoe joined the battalion of rangers, seized the heights (Husted's) and captured a captain and several men of the American light troops, but the main body escaped. The bodies of many of the Indians were buried in a small clearing in Van Cortlandt's woods, since known as the "Indian Field."

In July, 1781, Washington came in force to attempt a surprise of the British posts at King's Bridge, expressly to cut off De Lancey's and other light corps; but without success. Later in the month, accompanied by De Rochambeau, he moved a force of five thousand men down to the heights beyond King's Bridge and reconnoitered the northerly part of Manhattan island from Tippett's and Tetard's Hills and Fordham Heights. In September a British force of five thousand men moved out across the bridge to Valentine's Hill, as an escort to the young Prince William Henry. After the bitterly cold winter of 1782-83 the British troops were withdrawn from the Yonkers and King's Bridge. The inhabitants began to return to their desolate homes, while the Loyalists crowded into the city. In November, Washington came once more down the old post road, spent the night of the 12th at the Van Cortlandt house, and the next day, amid the acclamations of the people, rode victorious across King's Bridge, over which he had retreated seven years before.

POLITICAL HISTORY.—The area under consideration was part of the fief of Colen-donck from 1652 to 1664. After the English conquest in the latter year it belonged to the North Riding of Yorkshire until the erection of Westchester County under the act of October 1, 1691. It was afterwards known as the Yonkers Precinct (except the parts included in the Manor of Phillipsburgh after the erection of the latter, in 1693). By the act of June 19, 1703, the towns, manors, etc., were authorized to choose supervisors, and each inhabitant of any *precinct*, being a freeholder, was allowed "to join his vote with the next adjacent town." The freeholders of the Yonkers probably voted for a supervisor with the freeholders of East Chester. They chose their own local officers for the precinct, of whom the following "Collectors for the Yonkers" are known: William Jones, 1708–10; John Barrett, 1713–14; John Heading [Hadden], 1715–16; Mr. George Tippett, 1717; Mr. Joseph Taylor, 1718; Matthias Valentine, 1719; Joseph Hadley, 1720; Moses Taylor, 1721–23; William Jones, 1724; Moses Taylor, 1725; Thomas Sherwood, 1726; Moses Taylor, 1727; Thomas Rich, 1728; Edward Smith, 1729–30; Charles Vincent, 1731–32; Jacob Ryder, 1733–34; Joseph Taylor, 1736.

By the act of November 1, 1722, "to increase the number of supervisors for Westchester County," the inhabitants of each *precinct* having not less than twenty inhabitants were allowed to choose their own supervisor. The Yonkers was no doubt represented in the board by its own member thereafter; but by reason of the loss of the records of the precinct and of the board before 1772 their names are not known. On the first Tuesday in April, 1756, the freeholders and inhabitants of the Yonkers *and Mile Square*[1] held a public town-meeting at the house of Edward Stevenson, in the Yonkers, and chose James Corton (Corten ?) supervisor and pounder; Benjamin Fowler, town clerk; Thomas Sherwood, constable and collector; David Oakley and William Warner, assessors; Edward Weeks, Wm. Crawford, Daniel Devoe, John Ryder, Isaac Odell and Hendrick Post, highway masters; Andrew Nodine, Charles Warner, Moses Tailer and Isaac Odell, fence and damage viewers.[2]

Commissioners of highways in 1770: James Van Cortlandt and Benjamin Fowler.

Supervisors for the Yonkers: Colonel James Van Cortlandt, 1772-76; (none during the British occupation); Israel Honeywell, 1784; William Hadley, 1786-87; David Hunt, 1787.

Constables: Jeremiah Sherwood, 1773; Henry Odell, 1775; Thomas Sherwood, 1784.

By act of March 7, 1788, a new town was erected, containing part of Phillipsburgh, Mile Square and the old precinct of Yonkers, under the name of Yonkers. In November, 1872, the supervisors of

---

[1] It is probable that the Yonkers and Mile Square constituted one precinct under the name of the former. The Manor of Phillipsburgh surrounded Mile Square on three sides, and also separated it from the Yonkers. The inhabitants of the manor dwelling upon the old Mile Square road, between Yonkers and Mile Square, were sometimes described as "of the Yonkers in Phillipsburgh."

[2] Bolton's "Westchester County." The author must have seen the town-book (now, unfortunately, lost), and extracted the above from an account of the meeting of 1756.

KING'S BRIDGE.

Westchester County erected a township consisting of all of the town of Yonkers lying south of the southerly line of the city of Yonkers, to be called King's Bridge. Its first and only annual meeting was held at Temperance Hall, Mosholu, March 25, 1873. On the 1st of January, 1874, King's Bridge was annexed to the city of New York and now forms part of the Twenty-fourth Ward.

CHURCH HISTORY.—Before 1700 the inhabitants had no place of public worship nearer than East Chester. In 1707 they assembled "sometimes in the house of Joseph Betts, deceased, and sometimes in a barn when empty." About 1724 they had preaching three times a year by the rector from East Chester, and they "began to be in a disposition to build a church." None was erected, however, for more than a century. Those of the Reformed Dutch creed attended services at the church of Fordham Manor, erected in 1706. It stood on the northerly side of the road to Fordham Landing, where Moses Devoe's gateway now is. Upon the organization of the English Church at the Lower Mills those of that faith in the Yonkers attended there. After the Revolution Augustus Van Cortlandt and John Warner were of the first trustees of the new "Yonkers Episcopal Society," formed in 1787, and members of the first vestry of "St. John's Church in the town of Yonkers," on its incorporation, in 1795. Isaac Vermilye, William Hadley, William Warner and "Cobus" Dyckman were trustees of "the Reformed Dutch Church at the Lower Mills in the Manor of Phillipsburgh," incorporated in 1784.

METHODIST EPISCOPAL CHURCH BETHEL (Mosholu).—This was the first religious society to erect a house of worship in the limits of King's Bridge. So early as 1826 a charge existed, having thirty-six white members and one colored, under Samuel W. Fisher, preacher. Meetings were held in an old school-house which stood near Warner's store, Mosholu. In 1828 E. Hebard had the charge He remained during 1828 and organized a class. The succeeding preachers were R. Seaman, 1829-30; E. Hebard, 1831-32; E. Smith, 1833-34; Thomas Evans, 1835. On the 10th of February, 1835, Caleb Van Tassell, James Cole, Jacob Varian, Abraham Wood and John C. Lawrence were chosen trustees to build a church and February 14th Caleb Van Tassell and Jacob H. Varian made and filed a certificate of incorporation as "Trustees of Methodist Church Bethel" in the town of Yonkers. A frame building was erected on the westerly side of the Albany post road and is yet standing, though disused for several years. Its pastors have been E. Oldrin, I. D. Bangs and Thomas Barch (superannuated), 1836-37; John Davies, Salmon C. Perry and Barch, 1838; Henry Hatfield, Perry and Barch, 1839; Barch and Daniel I. Wright, 1840; Daniel I. Wright and Humphrey Humphreys, 1841; John A. Silleck and Humphreys, 1842; Silleck and Fred'k W. Seger, 1843; John C. Green and Mr. Barch, 1844-45; Charles C. Keyes, 1846-47; S. C. Perry, 1848-49; Paul R. Brown, 1850-51; Philip L. Hoyt, 1852; Richard Wheatly, 1853-54; Noble Lovett and Thos. Bainbridge, 1855; O. E. Brown and Bainbridge, 1856; A. B. Davis, 1857-58; R. H. Kelly, 1859-60; Wm. F. Browning and A. B. Brown, 1861; J. G. Shrive, 1862-63;

W. H. Smith, 1864; W. H. Smith, 1865; A. Ostrander, 1866-67; A. C. Gallahue, 1868; W. M. Henry, 1869; A. Ostrander, 1870; Wm. Plested, 1871; W. Tarleton, 1872; H. Croft, 1873; and Cyrus Nixon, 1874-75. Since that date the congregation has worshipped at King's Bridge.

CHURCH OF THE MEDIATOR (King's Bridge).—Formed at meeting held August 15, 1855, pursuant to notice given by the rector of St. John's Church, Yonkers, who presided. Certificate recorded November 17, 1856. Name adopted "The Church of the Mediator, Yonkers." Abraham Valentine and James R. Whiting were elected wardens, and Thomas J. De Lancey, William O. Giles, John C. Sidney, Russell Smith, Joseph H. Godwin, T. Bailey Myers, Daniel Valentine and David B. Cox, vestrymen. Certificate executed by Rev. A. B. Carter, A. Van Cortlandt and William O. Giles. The church, a frame structure, was erected on land presented by James R. Whiting at a cost of five thousand dollars, and the rectory on adjoining land soon afterwards. The church was consecrated by Bishop Horatio Potter November 6, 1864. The officiating clergyman in 1857 was Rev. T. James Brown, of the island of Jamaica. The rectors have been Rev. Cornelius W. Bolton, June, 1858, to May, 1859; Rev. Leigh Richmond Dickinson, June, 1859, to June, 1866; and Rev. William T. Wilson, since October, 1866.

RIVERDALE PRESBYTERIAN CHURCH.—Formed at a meeting held Wednesday, 24th June, 1863, Isaac G. Johnson and Edwin P. Gibson presiding. The first trustees chosen were Samuel N. Dodge, Robert Colgate, J. Joseph Eagleton, John Mott, James

Scrymser, Isaac G. Johnson, William E. Dodge, Jr Warren B. Sage and David B. Kellogg. Certificate of incorporation recorded July 14, 1863. The church building, of stone, was completed and dedicated October 11, 1863. Cost, about five thousand dollars. The stone parsonage adjoining was built soon after. The original membership was fifteen and the first elders were John Mott and Warren B. Sage. The pastors have been: George M. Boynton, October 28, 1863, to June, 1867; Henry H. Stebbins, August 25, 1867, to December 28, 1873, Charles H. Burr, March 5, 1874 to July 28, 1878; William R. Lord, April 30, 1879, to November 20, 1881; Ira S. Dodd, April 15, 1883, the present pastor. Entire membership, one hundred and twenty-five.

CHRIST CHURCH (Riverdale).—Formed at a meeting held September 10, 1866; Rev. E. M. Peck, chairman. Henry L. Stone and Newton Carpenter were elected wardens, and Samuel D. Babcock, George W. Knowlton, Thompson N. Hollister, Frederick Goodridge, Martin Bates, William W. Thompson, William H. Appleton and Henry F. Spaulding, vestrymen. Certificate by E. M. Peck, Percy R. Pyne and Charles H. P. Babcock, recorded September 15, 1866. Corporate name, "The Rector, Church Wardens and Vestrymen of Christ Church, Riverdale." The cornerstone of the church was laid in 1865. It is built of granitic gneiss and is cruciform. Rev. E. M. Peck acted as rector until the Rev. George D. Wildes, D.D., present rector, assumed charge, in 1868. The rectory adjoining the church is a frame building. There are some beautiful memorial windows in the church, notably one recently inserted by Percy R. Pyne at a cost of twenty-five thousand francs. It is a masterpiece of the French school by E. S. Oudinot and L. O. Merson, of Paris, representing the supper at Emmaus.

EDGE HILL CHAPEL (Spuyten Duyvil).—Erected in 1869, on land leased by Isaac G. Johnson at a nominal rent. Services are conducted every Sunday evening by the pastor of Riverdale Presbyterian Church.

WOODLAWN METHODIST EPISCOPAL CHURCH (Woodlawn Heights).—Organized in 1875. Building erected on lots donated by E. K. Willard; completed and dedicated April, 1876, by Bishop Janes. Pastors: D. W. C. Van Gaasbeek, 1875-76; Aaron Coons, 1876-79; Gustave Laws, 1880-81; J. O. Kern, 1881, present incumbent. Membership, thirty-nine.

ST. STEPHEN'S METHODIST EPISCOPAL CHURCH (King's Bridge).—Organized by trustees of the Methodist Episcopal Church Bethel (Mosholu) in 1875. Church completed and dedicated May 14, 1876. Pastors: D. W. C. Van Gaasbeek, 1875-76; Aaron Coons, 1876-79; David Tasker, 1879-80; S. Lowther, 1880-82; R. H. Kelly, 1882-83; Isaac H. Lent, present incumbent. Membership, forty-seven.

ST. JOHN'S CHURCH (King's Bridge).—Built under the direction of the Rev. Henry A. Brann, D.D., and dedicated December 3, 1880, by Cardinal McCloskey. Since its erection Dr. Brann has been aided in attending to the congregation by the Revs. Fr. Micena, Dr. Shrader, D. McCormick and William Fry, and the present assistant is Rev. Father O'Neill. Attached to the church are the St. John's Benevolent Society and St. Patrick's Temperance Society. The congregation numbers about five hundred souls and is connected with St. Elizabeth's Church, Fort Washington, where Dr. Brann resides.

VILLAGES.

King's Bridge.—The village of this name sprang up about thirty-five years ago, upon the ancient "island or hummock" of Paparinamin, from which it has since overspread the site of the old village of Fordham and the hillside beyond. Paparinamin was given, in 1668, by Elias Doughty to George Tippett. After his death, in 1675, Archer laid claim to it; but, exacting as a recognition of his manorial rights the annual payment of a "ffat capon" every New Year's day, he released the tract to Secretary Matthias Nicoll. Two years later Tippett's widow, then wife of Lewis Vitrey, reconveyed the island to Doughty, who, in turn, transferred it to the secretary. Thus the title to this tract vested in the colonial government, which had already assigned its use to Ferryman Verveelen. In 1693 it was included in the grant of the Manor of Phillipsburgh, of which it remained a part until forfeited by the attainder of Colonel Phillipse, in 1779. It was sold by the Commissioners of Forfeiture (deed July 30, 1785) to Joseph Crook, inn-keeper, Daniel Barkins and Abraham Lent, Jr., of Dutchess County, in joint tenancy. Medcef Eden, brewer, John Ramsey and Alexander von Pfister, merchants, subsequently owned it in whole or part; also, Daniel Halsey, inn-keeper, who kept the old tavern upon it between 1789 and 1793. It was purchased, 1797–99, from Von Pfister and Joseph Eden by Alexander Macomb, a wealthy merchant of New York.[1]

---

[1] Who purchased from the State in 1791 more than three

MACOMB'S DAM, HARLEM RIVER, 1850.

During the next five years Macomb purchased from Isaac Vermilye, John De Lancey, Isaac, John and Matthias Valentine, Andrew Corsa and Augustus Van Cortlandt adjoining parcels, mostly salt meadow, making up nearly one hundred acres, bounded north by Van Cortlandt, east by the Albany road, south by the Harlem and Spuyten Duyvil, and west by Tippett's Brook. Having obtained from the mayor, etc., of New York, in December, 1800, a water grant extending across the creek, just east of the King's Bridge (which reserved, however, a passage-way fifteen feet wide for small boats and craft), Macomb erected a four-story frame grist-mill extending out over the creek. Its power was supplied by the alternate ebb and flow of the tide against its under-shot wheel. Macomb's extensive real estate ventures proving disastrous, Paparinamin and the mill were sold under foreclosure in 1810, and purchased by his son Robert. By an act of 1813 the latter was authorized to construct a dam across the Harlem from Bussing's to Devoe's Point, and to use the water for milling purposes, and erected at much expense the causeway and bridge known as "Macomb's Dam." Its gates admitted the flood tide from the East River, but obstructed its ebb, thus converting the Upper Harlem into a mill-pond, having its outlets underneath the old mill and through a raceway made on the Westchester side into Spuyten Duyvil Creek at low tide. The race supplied power to a marble-sawing mill which stood on a quay between it and the creek, and

---

five hundred thousand acres in Northern New York, at 8d. per acre. The Adirondack Mountains were long known as "Macomb's Mountains."

KING'S BRIDGE.

of which Perkins Nicolls was proprietor. Robert Macomb becoming involved, the property was sold by the sheriff in 1818. Ten years later it was possessed by the "New York Hydraulic Manufacturing and Bridge Company," by which an elaborate plan was put forth for mill-seats and a manufacturing village, based on a report of Professor James Renwick, of Columbia College, approved by Colonel Totten and General Macomb, chief engineers United States army. The enterprise proved abortive.[1] The old gristmill[2] stood idle during many years, and at length was made useless by the removal of Macomb's Dam. In 1830 Mary C. P. Macomb, the wife of Robert, acquired the Paparinamin tract, and during many years made the old stone tavern her home, exercising therein a generous hospitality, of which Edgar Allen Poe was a frequent recipient. In 1847 Mrs. Macomb laid out the estate into streets and plots, which she afterwards disposed of. Several houses were erected, stores and shops were opened, a church built and a centre of population established, which has grown to several hundreds. There are now three churches, a grammar school, police station, numerous stores, shops, saloons and dwellings. Among the

---

[1] It was proposed, in an elaborate prospectus, to dam the Yonkers River (Tippett's Brook) near its mouth, and have gates opening down-stream only. The bed of the stream and the salt meadows through which it flowed were to form a reservoir for tail-water, which would empty itself into Spuyten Duyvil Creek at low tide. Fourteen mill-seats, each fifty by one hundred feet, bordered the race-ways, and an aggregate of at least two hundred and thirty-four horse-power was assured for mills.

[2] It fell down about 1856.

well-known residents are Joseph H. Godwin,[1] William G. Ackerman, William O. Giles, George Moller, William A. Varian, M.D., Benjamin T. Sealey, William H. Geer, John Parsons, M.D., Rev. William T. Wilson and others.

SPUYTEN DUYVIL.—A village (and until recently a post office) located on the southerly end of Spuyten Duyvil Neck. The land was owned by George Tippett, who died in 1761. He devised it in several parcels to his children and grandchildren. Soon after the Revolution it belonged to Samuel Berrien, who had married Dorcas Tippett, daughter of George.[2] He sold to Abraham Berrien, a nephew, in whose family it continued until about 1850. In 1852 the tract was in three farms, which were purchased that year and next by Elias Johnson, David B. Cox and Joseph W. Fuller, of Troy, N. Y. They had surveys and plans made for a village to be called Fort Independence,[3] but which was changed to Spuyten Duyvil. Streets were opened and several houses erected on the hill, and a foundry was established at its base. The latter was afterwards bought and extended into a rolling-mill by Jervis Langdon, who was succeeded by the Langdon Rolling-Mill Company. The Spuy-

---

[1] Mr. Godwin's residence is the old Macomb mansion, now altered and enlarged.

[2] A grandson of the first proprietor of the name. His wife was Dorcas ———. He had sons: George, William, James and Thomas (all of whom married and had issue), and daughters: Jane, wife of Charles Warner; Phebe, wife of George Hadley; and Dorcas, wife of Samuel Berrien. The Rev. William Berrien, rector of Trinity Parish, New York, and its historian, was a grandson of the latter.

[3] After the Revolutionary fort, erroneously supposed to have occupied this hill.

ten Duyvil Rolling-Mill Company, organized in 1867, next owned this property. A malleable iron foundry was established on adjoining premises by Isaac G. Johnson and now employs several hundred hands. There are about thirty private dwellings on the elevated ground, including the residences of Mrs. D. B. Cox, Thomas H. Edsall, George C. Holt, Isaac G. Johnson,[1] Elias Johnson, Gilbert Johnson, Henry R. Lounsbery, David M. Morrison, George H. Petrie, Albert E. Putnam, Joseph R. Sergeant, Mrs. Peter O. Strang, Warren B. Sage, Henry M. Smith and others.

Immediately northward is a tract of three hundred and fifty-six acres, also known as Spuyten Duyvil. Frederick Van Cortlandt purchased it in several parcels between 1768 and 1788, and built his house on a commanding spot on the easterly side, approached by a private road leading up from the post road at Mosholu. He devised this property to his brother Augustus, by whose will it passed to a grandson, Augustus F. Morris, who assumed the name of Van Cortlandt. From him James R. Whiting bought the tract in 1836 and about 1840 erected a large stone mansion on the western side, overlooking the Hudson. Samuel Thomson, William C. Wetmore and Daniel Ewing became interested in Whiting's purchase in 1841, and they subsequently divided it into parcels stretching from the Hudson across the neck to Tippett's Brook. Thomson took the northerly parcel, on which stood a large stone house erected about 1822

---

[1] Mr. Johnson resides in the old Berrien house, which he has enlarged and improved.

on the site of the "Upper Cortlandts'," destroyed in
that year by fire. Surrounded by well laid out and
highly-improved grounds, it is now the residence of
Waldo Hutchins. Near by is Hiram Barney's beautiful country-seat, "Cedar Knolls." The Whiting
mansion is occupied by James R. Whiting, Jr. Adjoining is the house of James A. Hayden. The late
General John Ewen's country-seat on this tract is
now occupied by his widow.

HUDSON PARK was laid out in 1853, on the westerly
part of Samuel Thomson's tract. A single house on
the river-side was the only one erected for many
years. There is now a cluster of small dwellings
known as "Cooperstown," on this tract.

North of Hudson Park, and extending across from
the Hudson to the Albany road, was the old Hadley
farm of two hundred and fifty-seven acres, of which
William Hadley died seized in 1802. He purchased
the southerly part, about one hundred and fifty acres
extending up to the line of the Manor of Phillipsburgh, from James Van Cortlandt, in 1761, and the
remainder from the Commissioners of Forfeiture, May
18, 1786. He lived in the old stone house yet standing on this tract, just west of the post road. Joseph
Delafield purchased the farm from Hadley's executors in 1829, and it is now owned by Delafield's
children and grandchildren. The residence of Maturin
L. Delafield is on the west side of Riverdale Avenue.
The house of the late Lewis L. Delafield stands on
the brow of the hill overlooking the Hudson. Mr.
William E. Dodge's country-seat is on this tract. On
the west side of Riverdale Avenue is a new fire-engine
house, the first erected in the old Yonkers. Its tower

contains a melodious old Spanish bell, cast in 1762 by Llonart.

RIVERDALE.—A village (and until recently a post-office) situated on part of Phillipsburgh Manor, which was sold by the Commissioners of Forfeiture to George Hadley, December 6, 1785. In 1843 William G. Ackerman acquired about one hundred acres of this tract, part of which was purchased in 1853 by W. W. Woodworth, H. L. Atherton, Samuel D. Babcock and C. W. Foster, and laid out as the village of Riverdale. In 1856 Henry F. Spaulding and others laid out the land adjoining on the south as "The Park, Riverdale." On these lands have since been erected a number of beautiful country-houses, including those of William H. Appleton, Samuel D. Babcock, Martin Bates, George H. Bend, Robert Colgate, William S. Duke, R. L. Franklin, George H. Forster, Frederick Goodridge, Laura Harriman, D. Willis James, Percy R. Pyne, Moses Taylor Pyne, Henry F. Spaulding, H. L. Stone and others. There are two churches and a school-house, but no places of business in Riverdale.[1]

MT. ST. VINCENT AND THE SISTERS OF CHARITY.—In the northwest corner of what was formerly the town of King's Bridge, lying along the Hudson River, and partly jutting over the northern boundary of the city of New York into the adjoining city of Yonkers, is Mount St. Vincent—the property of the Sisters of Charity—a picturesque tract of more than fifty acres of land, together with the convent and other build-

---

[1] Between Riverdale and Mount St. Vincent is a part of the old John Warner farm, formerly owned by A. Schermerhorn, and another part owned by J. E. Bettner, E. F. Brown and others. Some fine stone country-houses have recently been erected on these tracts.

ings which make the mother house of the Sisters in the Archdiocese of New York. The institution was founded here in 1856, when this site was still in Westchester County. Nearly a thousand Sisters, in more than a hundred subordinate houses, including asylums, hospitals, the Girls' Protectory in Westchester, the retreat for the insane at Harrison, industrial schools, academies and parish schools, are governed from Mt. St. Vincent. The many parish and other schools, under the Sisters of Charity from this house, and situated in Westchester County and in and near New York, include about thirty-five thousand pupils, besides the hundreds of sick and infirm in their different asylums and hospitals.

The Sisters of Charity are a benevolent corporation of women only, formed under the general laws of the State of New York, and governed by their own trustees elected from among themselves, and are largely independent. The Mother Superior is the president of the corporation. Mother Angela Hughes, the youngest sister of Archbishop Hughes, was superior of the order when the Sisters, in December, 1856, bought this property of Edwin Forrest, with the farm buildings and the castle upon it, as he had built them for his own residence.[1] The following year Mother Angela commenced the new building, which now forms the central part of the present convent, overlooking the Hudson, between two and three hundred yards distant. This first building, with a

[1] The Forrest property was part of the large farm that Captain John Warner, of the Revolutionary army, bought at the sale of the confiscated estate of Colonel Frederick Phillipse.—*Deed of Commissioners of Forfeiture*, Dec. 6, 1785.

front of two hundred and seventy feet, has by later additions been enlarged to more than five hundred feet of frontage, making a handsome brick structure, three stories in height, with high basement and attic and a lofty spire.

Mother Angela's term of office expired in 1862 since which date Mother Jerome and Mother Regina have successively ruled the order. Mother Angela died in 1866, Mother Regina in 1879 and Mother Jerome in 1885, since which date Sister M. Ambrosia, who, twenty-five years before, had been in charge of the girls' parish school in Yonkers, then treasurer at Mt. St. Vincent, and subseqently the head of the Girls' Protectory at Westchester, and later assistant-mother at Mt. St. Vincent, has been the Mother Superior there.

The south half of the convent building contains the Academy of Mt. St. Vincent, a girls' school of the highest class, numbering between two and three hundred pupils, with the philosophical apparatus and the appointments of a college. The pupils are divided into many classes, each class under the immediate charge of a Sister specially selected for her natural endowments and careful training. Sister Maria (Mary C. Dodge)[1] has long been the directress of the academy, subordinate to the Mother Superior. The academic course runs through four years, preceded by a preparatory school for those who need it, and followed by a post-graduate course.

The north half of the convent is the mother house of the Sisters, the residence of the Mother Superior

---

[1] Authoress of an interesting history of the institution.

and her assistants, with the Sisters of the academy, as well as those at home from the outside missions for needed rest or in broken health, so that there are usually a hundred Sisters or more in the house. At the extreme north end is now the spacious novitiate, built in 1885. The institution has a hundred novices in a two years' course of training and probation under the Mother of Novices, and there are usually a dozen or twenty candidates for the novitiate awaiting admission through three months or more of probation.

The convent chapel, as large as a parish church, is in an extension to the east, nearly in the middle of the convent, between the Sisters' department and that of the pupils. The convent has a large number of fine paintings and works of art, and everything about the building is admirable for its neatness and good order, and the extensive grounds are always well kept. The carriage drive from the convent to the eastern entrance at Riverdale Avenue is about half a mile in length, and towards the west, on the Hudson, a quarter of a mile from the convent door, is the Mt. St. Vincent Station of the New York Central and Hudson River Railroad, on the Sisters' own grounds. The institution is supplied with gas and with water from the Yonkers works, and is under the protection of the New York City police. The picturesque stone castle of Edwin Forrest still stands between the convent and the railroad station, and a part is made the dwelling of the chaplain of the institution. The larger rooms on the first floor are occupied by the museum of natural history, the collection of minerals being unusually large and good,[1] and there is also a fine cabinet of coins and medals.[2]

On their own ground, on a side-street near Riverdale Avenue, the Sisters, in 1875, built, at a cost of over twenty thousand dollars, "St Vincent's Free School," a brick building sixty by ninety feet, where they continue to teach, at their own cost, a free primary school now numbering about one hundred and fifty boys and girls of the vicinity.

The residences of Edmund D. Randolph and Mr. B. Cuthbert adjoin this property on the south.

MOSHOLU[3] is an old hamlet and post-office skirting the Albany post road, known early in the century as "Warner's," where many years ago there were a church (Methodist), school-house, store, blacksmith and wagon-shop and a cluster of dwellings.

WOODLAWN HEIGHTS.—A village (and until recently a post-office) on the Harlem Railroad, laid out in 1873 by George Opdyke and others on a part of the old Gilbert Valentine farm, in the Yonkers. E. K. Willard extended the village northward the same year to the Mile Square road, on land formerly part of Phillipse Manor. A church and a number of small dwelling-houses have been erected on these plots.

VAN CORTLANDT'S is a station on the New York City and Northern Railroad, located near the old Van Cortlandt pond and mills. Near by are the ice-houses and residence of George R. Tremper. The historic old mansion (1748), now the residence of Augustus Van Cortlandt, stands a few hundred yards

---

[1] Presented by Dr. E. S. F. Arnold, of New York.
[2] Forrest purchased this estate in 1847, and called it "Font Hill."
[3] So called after the Indian name of Tippett's Brook.

northward, upon Van der Donck's ancient planting-field. Opposite to the car-houses, beyond the station is an ancient burial-place, probably that of the Betts and Tippett families in the seventeenth century.

OLAFF PARK is a name given to about one hundred acres of the Van Cortland's estate, purchased and laid out in 1869 by W. N. Woodworth, and so called after the name of the ancestor of the Van Cortlandts in America. No improvements have been made on this tract except to open streets and avenues.

WOODLAWN CEMETERY.—This beautiful "city of the dead" consists of about four hundred acres on the heights of the Bronx, extending westward to an ancient road, whose line is now followed by Central Avenue. The house of Abraham Vermilye stood on its easterly side in 1781. Early in this century John Bussing, Daniel Tier, William and Abraham Valentine owned the farms of which the cemetery is now composed. The cemetery was organized in December, 1863, and the improvement of the grounds commenced in April, 1864. The first interment was made January 14, 1865, since which time there have been upwards of twenty-six thousand burials therein.

RAILROADS.—The earliest was the New York and Harlem, along the easterly bounds, chartered May 12, 1831; opened to Harlem, 1837, and to White Plains, 1844. For nearly thirty years the nearest station was at Williams' Bridge. There is one now at Woodlawn. The Hudson River Railroad, chartered April 25, 1831, was opened along the westerly bounds of the district about 1850. Stations: Spuyten Duyvil, Riverdale and Mount St. Vincent. The Spuyten Duyvil and Port Morris Railroad, chartered April 24, 1867, was opened in 1871. Stations: Spuyten Duyvil and King's Bridge. The New York City and Northern Railroad was reorganized and opened in 1878. Stations: King's Bridge and Van Cortlandt's.

AQUEDUCTS.—1. The Croton aqueduct, begun 1837 and completed 1842, passes along the brow of Valentine's, Gun and Tetard's Hills. 2. The Bronx River water supply, determined upon in 1879 and opened September 9, 1884, is carried in a forty-eight-inch cast-iron conduit pipe along the west side of the Bronx to Woodlawn and thence to the top of the hill, half a mile west of Williams' Bridge Station, where a distributing reservoir is located and whence thirty-six inch pipes distribute the water to the Twenty-third and Twenty-fourth Wards. 3. The new Croton supply, determined upon in 1884 and work in progress, will go near the old one, mostly through rock tunnel. 4. Mt. St. Vincent, Riverdale and Spuyten Duyvils have been supplied from Yonker water-works since 1882.

SCHOOLS.—The most ancient was the French boarding-school of Dominie Tetard, opened in 1772. Early in the century there was a school-house near Warner's store and another on the Mile Square road, near Devoe's. The school-house at Mosholu (now Grammar No. 67) was erected about 1840. The one at King's Bridge (now. Grammar School No. 66) was erected in 1872. The one at Spuyten Duyvil (now Primary No. 44) was erected about 1859. Primary No. 48, at Woodlawn, was established in 1880. The Riverdale Institute, a seminary for young ladies, and the boarding-school for boys at Hudson Park have been closed for several years. The academy at Mount St. Vincent is mentioned under that head.

APPENDIX.

THE O'NEALE PATENT.

A Patent graunted unto Mr. Hugh Oneb, and Mary his wife.

Richard Nicolls Esq'r' Governour under his Royall Highnesse, the Duke of Yorke, of all his Territoryes in America, To all to whom these presents shall come, sendeth Greeting; Whereas there is a certaine Tract of Land within this Governm't upon the Maine, Bounded to the Northwards by a Rivolett called by the Indyans Maccakassin, so running Southward to Nepperhane from thence to the Kill Shorakkapock, and then to Papiriniman, which is the Southermost Bounds, then to go Crosse the Country to the Eastward, by that which is commonly knowne by the name of Bronckx his River, and Land, which said Tract of Land, hath heretofore beene Purchased of the Indyan Proprietors by Adrian Vander Duncke, deceased, whose Relict, Mary the wife of Hugh Oneale, one of the Patentees is, and due Satisfaccon was also given for the same, as hath by some of the said Indyans, beene Acknowledged before mee; Now for a further Confirmacon unto them the said Hugh Oneale and Mary his wife, Relict of the aforesaid Adrian Vancker Duncke, in their Possession and Enjoyment of the premises,

APPENDIX.

Know ye that by vertue of the Commission and Authority given unto mee by his Royall Highnesse, the Duke of Yorke, I have thought fitt to Give, Ratify, Confirme and Grannt, And by these presents do Give, Ratify Confirme and Grannt unto the said Hugh Oneale and Mary his wife, their heyres & assignes all the afore mentioned Parcell or Tract of Land called Nepperhane Together with all woods, Marshes, Meadowes Pastures waters, Lakes, Creekes, Rivoletts, ffishing, Hunting and ffowling. And all other Profitts, Commodities and Emoluments, to the said Tract of Land belonging, with their and every of their Appurtenances, and of every part and Parcell thereof ; To have and to hold the said Tract of Land and pr'misses, with all and Singular their Appurtenances, unto the said Hugh Oneale and Mary his wife, their Heires and Assignes, to the proper use and behoofe of the send Hugh Oneale, and Mary his wife, their Heires and Assignes for ever, Hee, shee or they or any of them, Rendring and Paying such Acknowledgments and Dutyes, as are or shall bee Constituted and Ordained, by his Royall Highnesse ye Duke of Yorke and his Heires, or such Governour and Governo'rs as shall from time to time be appointed and sett over them ; with this Proviso, That if at any time hereafter, his Royall Highnesse, his Heires, Successors or Assignes, shall thinke fitt to make use of any Timber for Shipping, or for Erecting or repairing of fforts within this Government, a Liberty is reserved for such uses and purposes, to Cutt any sorts of Timber, upon any Implanted Grounds, on the said Tract of Land, to make Docks, Harbors, Wharfes, Houses, or any other conveniencies relating there unto, And also to make use of any Rivers, Rivoletts and Inletts of Water, to the purposes aforesd as fully and freely, as if no such Patent had beene grannted; Given under my hand and Seale, at ffort James in New Yorke, on the Island of Manhatans, the Eighth day of October, in the Eighteenth yeare of the Raigne of our Sovereigne Lord, Charles the Second, by the grace of God, of England, Scotland, ffrance and Ireland King, Defender of the ffaith &c, And in the yeare of our Lord God 1666.

RICHARD NICOLLS.

ASSIGNMENT, O'NEALE AND WIFE TO ELIAS DOUGHTY.

[Indorsed on the Patent.]

These Presents wittnesse that I Hugh Oneale with the Consent of Mary my Wife Doe Assigne and sett over unto my Brother in Law Elias Doughty of fflushing in the County of Yorkshire on Long Island his heirs and Assignes for Ever all my whole Right title and Interest belonging to me and Mary my wife menConed in this Pattent as wittnesse my hand this thirtith Day of october 1666 Acknowledging hereby to have Received full Sattisfaction for the same the Day and yeare Aforesaid.

HUGH ONEALE.
MARY ONEALE.

Testis Edward flisher, John Oksanne.

ASSIGNMENT, DOUGHTY TO DELAVALL, PHILLIPS AND LEWIS.

[Indorsed on the Patent.]

I doe hereby Assigne and Transporte all my Right Title and Interest to the within written Pattent and

APPENDIX.

Premisses unto Thomas Delavall Esq'r' ffredrick Phillips Merch't and Tho. Lewis Marriner for A Valuable Consideraͤon. In witnesse whereof I have hereunto Sett my hand & seale this 29th Day of March 1672.

ELYAS DOUGHTY (seal).

Sealed Delivered & acknowledged before me Matthias Nicolls, Ferry'm. [Sec'y.]

John Sharpe.

[The above assignment, while it purports to transfer the "Pattent and Premisses," did not convey the whole of the latter, prior transfers of portions of the land having been made by Doughty, to Archer, Betts & Tippett, and Hadden, *ut sub.*]

DEED, ELIAS DOUGHTY TO JOHN ARCHER.

Recorded for Mr. John Arch'r this 24th day of September, Anno Dm 1671.

Know all Men by these pr'sents that I Elyas Doughty of Flushing doe sell unto Mr. John Archer of West-Chest'r his Heyres & Assigns ffourescore Acres of Upland, and thirty Acres of Meadow lyeing & being betwixt Brothers River and the Wateing Place at ye End of the Island of Manhatans, and if ye Land be not fitt to Cleare for ye Plow or How, this Land is to lye together; And if there be not all such Land together as there should, or if there should happen to be eight or ten Acres of Land that is not fitt for such Use, Then ye said Archer is to have it with ye rest, and hee shall have equall Right and Privilege in ye Commons as any of their Men shall have within that Patent, that hath noe more

APPENDIX.

Arable Land, and ye Meadow is to be mowed all As Witness my Hand this first of March 1666. As Wittness if there should lye any more Land, that is to say between ffourty or thirty Acres, It is all in Common; And I am to give ye said Archer a firme Bill of Sale under my Hand and Seale.

ELIAS DOUGHTY.
THOMAS OKELEY.

I Elias Doughty doe own to have received full Satisfaction of ye said Archer for ye said Land & Meadow ye House is yett to be And ye said Arch'r is to have his   within the above said Tract of Land.

Septemb'r ye 18th 1667.

It is to be understood that Mr. John Archer is to have the ffreshest Boggy Meadow that lyeth on ye South side of Westchester Path, within ye Patent of Mr. Oneale within his second of Purchase w'ch is upon Consideracon that ye said John Archer shall pay to ye said Doughty; As Witness my Hand

ELYAS DOUGHTY.

DEED, ELIAS DOUGHTY TO WILLIAM BETTS AND GEORGE TIPPETT.

Recorded for George Tippett ffeb'ry 22th 1670.

Be it knowne unto all men by theise pr'sents that I Elias Doughty of fflushing in ye North Ryding of Yorkshire on Long Island in America w'thin ye Territoryes of his R. H'ss ye Duke of Yorke and'r ye Command of ye Rt. Hon'ble Co'l Richard Nicolls Governo'r Gen'r'll of ye same have by vertue of ye Assignation of a Pattent from my brother in Law

APPENDIX.

Mr. Hugh Oneale & Mary his wife alienated estranged demised bargained & sould & do by theise pr'sents alyenate estrauge demise bargaine & sell a parte & parcell of that Land & meadow belonging to ye said Pattent for & in consideration of a considerable sume received & to receive w'ch land & meadow I the abovesaid Doughty have sold unto William Betts & George Tippett who are possest of parte of ye same (viz't) ye said Land & meadowe w'ch was formerly in ye possession & occupation of old Youncker van der Dounckx ye planting feild belonging to ye said Purchase to be of ye North syde of ye said purchase, ye marked trees making mention of ye same, & w'ch rune west to Hudsons Ryver & East to Broncke his Ryver w'ch all ye Upland from Bronx his Ryver Southward to Westchester path, & so runs due East & West beginning at ye boggy Swamp w'thin ye Libertye of ye said Pattent & ye Southwardmost bounds to run by ye path that runneth or lyeth by ye North end of ye aforesaid Swamp & so to run due East to Broncks his Ryver & due west to that meadowe w'ch cometh from ye wading place, w'ch all ye meadowe from ye Stake w'ch is on ye Eastward syde of the abovesaid wading place w'ch is now in controversy betweene me ye abovesaid Doughty & some Inhabitants w'thin Harlem, w'ch all ye Meadow betwixt the abovesaid Stake Eastward & Hudsons Ryver Westward from ye abovesaid wading place at ye Nithermost end of Manhatans Island, w'th all ye Upland betwixt that & Hudsons River westward & so running northward to ye East & West lyne before mentioned at ye end of ye planting field except ye thirty Acres of

APPENDIX.

meadowe w'th I have sold unto Mr. John Archer w'ch ye abovesaid Betts and Tippett is to be pfourmed unto ye abovesaid John Archer, & for that parcell of meadowe w'ch is now in Controversy betweene ye Harlem men & myselfe if it be recovered by them or their order they shall peaceably enjoy ye Same according to ye Tenor of ye Pattent paying unto me or my order Ten pounds of Current passable pay according to ye custome of theise partes, & in Case ye same due shall be recovered then Mr. John Archer his proportion of Thirty Acres of Meadowe is to run upward by ye Island where he is to have ye full complement of yo said Thirty Acres. All w'ch I have from myselfe my heires or any oth'r p'son or p'sons interested or concerned in ye said Pattent Sold & made over unto ye afore mentioned William Betts & George Tippett or eith'r of them their heires Executors or Assigns To have & to hold for ever, & ye same peaceably & quietly to enjoy maintaining ye Same free from all Incumbrances of any p'son or p'sons concerned in ye Pattent Indians Excepted, It is to be understood that Mr. Archers Meadowe is to be laid out in Case Harlem men enjoy their possession at ye Stake parting ye said meadowe in controversye & ye other meadowe w'ch I have possest them of, In witnes whereof I have hereunto sett my hand and Seale this 6th Day of July Anno Dm. 1668 & in ye 20th yeare of ye Raigne of o'r Sovereigne Lord Charles ye Second by ye Grace of God of England Scotland ffrance & Ireland King Defender of ye faith &c.   ELIAS DOUGHTY
Signed Sealed & delivered in ye pr'sence of us JOHN HOLDEN, JOHN HADON, JOHN MARSHALL.

APPENDIX.

DEED, ELIAS DOUGHTY TO JOHN HADDEN.

Recorded for Jno. Heddy, Sept. 26th 1672.

Bee it known unto all Men by these Presents that I Elyas Doughty of ffushing in the North Riding of York-shire on Long Island in America w'thin ye Territoryes of his Royall Highness the Duke of Yorke, under ye Command of the Right Hon'ble Coll. Richard Nicolls Governor Gen'all of the same, by vertue of the Assignacon of a Patent from my Brother in Law Mr. Henry Oneale & Mary his Wife, have alienated, estranged, demised, bargained, & sold, & doe by these Presents alienate, estrange, demise, bargaine & sell unto John Heddy late of West-Chester w'thin the Riding, & Government above mencioned two hundred Acres of Vpland belonging to the said Patent, to beginn at ye North-side of the Planting ffield, where ye abovesaid John Heddy shall see most convenient; viz't to beginn at the West, & runn towards the East, the length & breadth thereof to bee as the Purchaser shall see most Comodious; w'ch is for and in consideracon of full Satisfaction already received by a Horse; And further I the said Elyas Doughty doe make over and deliver unto the said John Heddy twenty Acres more of Vpland adjoyning to the abovesaid two hundred, w'ch is all to beginn at the Northside of the Planting ffield belonging to William Betts and George Tippett from ye West end of the Land, & to runn in length Eastward towards Broncks River; And further I the abovesaid Elyas Doughty have sold unto the abovesaid Jno. Heddy one hundred Acres more of Vpland, lying and being in the aforesaid Range for & in consideracon of five pounds to paid upon Bill according to Agreement ; All w'ch I Elyas Doughty have sold & made over from mee my Heyres & Executors to ye said Heddy his Heyres, Executors, Administrators or Assignes ; To have and to hold forever ; Maintaining the same free from any Incumbrances that may or shall hereafter arise from any Person or Persons laying any Clayme or Title to the same, Interested in ye above-mentioned Patent.

In Wittness to w'ch I have hereunto sett my Hand and Seale this 7th day of June in ye yeare of the Reigne of our Soveraigne Lord Charles ye 2d by the Grace of God, King of England, Scotland, France & Ireland, Defender of the ffaith &c :

ELIAS DOUGHTY (Seale).

Signed Sealed & Delivered in the pr'sence of us,

his
GEORGE / TIPPETT.
mark

JOHN HOLDEN.
WM. BETTS.   JNO. MARSHALL.

Endorsed on ye Deed as followeth. These may Certify, that ye within mentioned three hundred & twenty eight Acres of Land, is layd out as followeth ; Inprimis, Twenty eight Acres lyeing in one piece, beginning from the Market tree of Wm. Betts & George Tippett, from thence running due North 24 Chayne in length ; & in breadth due East 20 chayne, being bounded on the South w'th the Land of Wm. Betts & George Tippett, & to ye Northward Westward by ye Land of Capt' Delavall ; the other two hundred ninety two Acres beginning at ye Eastward end of the twenty eight Acres, Running in length due East Eighty Chayne, & in breadth due North Thirty six Chayne & fifty Lincks, being bounded to ye Southward by the Lands of Wm. Betts & George Tippett; & to ye Eastward, Northward, & Westward by ye Lands of Capt' De Lavall; w'ch aforemenĉoned Land was survey'd & layd out by mee as afore exprest. Given under my Hand this 3d day of September 1672.

ROBERT RIDER.

DEED, ELIAS DOUGHTY TO DELAVALL AND OTHERS.

To all Christian People to whom this Present writeing shall Come Elyas Doughty of fflushing in North Rydeing of Yorkeshire upon Long Island sendeth Greeting in our Lord God Everlasting whereas the said Elyas Doughty Standeth possest of A considerable porĉon of a Certaine Tract or parcell of Land upon the Maine Continent within this his Roy'll High'ss his Governm't Commonly Called the Younckers Land for the which their was a Pattent graunted by the late Governor Coll Rich'd Nicolls unto Hugh Oneale and Mary his Wife who was the widdow and Relict of Adrian Vander Dunck by Virtue whereof an Assignm't and Transporte of their whole Right Title and Interest was for a Valuable Consideraĉon made by the said Hugh Oneale and Mary his Wife unto the said Elyas Doughty his heires and Assignes together with the Originall Pattent and all the Privilidges and Perquisites thereunto belonging; now know yee that the said Elyas Doughty for and in Consideraĉon of the sume of Eighty pounds or goods to the value thereof att mony price in hand payed or secured to be paid att

APPENDIX.

or before the Ensealeing and Delivery hereof by Thomas Delavall of the City of New Yorke Esq'r Fredrick Phillips of the same Citty March't and Thomas Lewis of the same place Marrin'r Doth hereby Acknowledge and thereof Doth acquit Exonerate and Discharge them the said Thom. Delavall, Fredrick Phillips and Thomas Lewis their heirs Executors and Adminis'tors hath given graunted, Aliened, bargained, Sold, Ensealed & confirmed and by these Presents Doth fully Cleerly and Absolutely give grant alien bargaine sell and Confirme unto the said Thomas Delavall ffredrick Phillips and Thomas Lewis their heires Executors Adm'r'tors and Assigne s for ever all the Remaineing parte of that Tract or Parcell of Land in his Disposall within the Limitts and precincts of the Pattent Aforemenconed, Excepting only out of the Generall Pattent Aforesaid within the Lymitts and precincts of the Patent Aforemenconed Excepting only out of the Generall Pattent afores'd what is herein Excepted That is to say A parcell of Land Sold by him the said Elyas Doughty Vnto John Archer his heyres and Assignes another parcell neare Adjoyneing, sold unto Wm. Betts George Tippett and John Heddy as alsoe A Mile square of Land within the said Pattent by Broncks River near East Chester sold unto some of the Inhabitants of that place, All which said parcells are perticulerly sett forth with their Buttings and Boundings in the Respective Bills of Sale Signed and Delivered by the said Elyas Doughty to the said persons Concerned, And likewise the said Elyas Doughty Doth hereby Assigne and transporte all his Right title and Interest to the remaineing parte

APPENDIX.

of the said Pattent together with the original Pattent and all Deeds Writeings and Escripts Concerning the same unto the same Thomas De Lavall ffredrick Phillips and Thomas Lewis their heires Executors Adm'st'ors and Assignes as alsoe all the Rights Royaltyes Privilidges Immunityes and Proffits thereunto belonging or in any wise appertaineing in as ample manner as hee himselfe or the said Hugh Oneale and Mary his Wife held the same, To have and To hold the said Land and Premmisses hereby granted bargained & Sold with their and every of their Rights proffitts and Appurtenances unto the said Thomas Delavall Fredrick Phillips and Thomas Lewis their heires and Assignes unto the proper use and behoofe of them the said Thomas Delavall Fredrick Phillips and Thomas Lewis their heires and Assignes for ever. And the said Elyas Doughty for himselfe his heires Executors Adm'r'tors and for every of them Doth Covenant Promisse & Grant to and with the said Thomas Delavall Fredrick Phillips and Thomas Lewis their heires Executors Adm'r'tors and Assignes and to and w'th every of them, that they the said Thomas Delavall Fredrick Phillips and Thomas Lewis their heires and Assignes shall and may from henceforth for ever peaceably and quietly have hold use Occupy, possesse and Enjoye the said Land and premisses before Recited, (excepted what is herein Excepted) without the Lett Interrupcon or Contradiccon of him the said Elyas Doughty his heires or Assignes or of any p'rson or p'rsons Clayming from by or under him, them or any of them; And that the said Land is and shall be quitt and ffree from any Incumbrance of Dowry or Joynture Mort-

gage, or former Grant, or Sale other then what 1
herein exprest and shall make good the same with
Warranty ag't all other p'rsons whatsoever. In Te-
timony Whereof hee the said Elyas Doughty Hath
hereunto Putt his hand and Seale the twenty ninth
Day of November in the twenty fourth Yeare of the
Reigne of our Sovereigne Lord Charles the Second
by the Grace of God of England Scotland ffrance
and Irel'd King Defend'r of the ffaith &c A'o D.
1672.

Sealed and Delivered in the pr'sence of Matthias
Nicolls, John Sharpe.

ELYAS DOUGHTY (Seale).

BETTS AND TIPPETT PATENT.

A Confirmaton of a Certaine Parcell of Land upon
ye Maine Granted to Wm. Betts & George Tippett.

Francis Lovelace Esq'r' &c Whereas Elyas Doughty
of ffiushing hath for a Valuable Consideration by
Bill of Sale bearing date ye 6th day of July 1668
convey'd & made over unto Wm. Betts & George
Tippett late of West Chester a Certaine parcell or
Tract of Land upon ye Maine being part of a Greater
Quantity heretofore belonging to Adriaen Vand'r
Donck & Granted by Patent from Governo'r Nicolls
to Hugh Oneale & Mary his Wife who was ye Widdow
& Relict of ye said Vander Donck & from them Con-
vey'd together w'th all their Title & Interest in ye
Premisses unto ye aboves'd Elyas Doughty his
Heyres & Assignes'; The said Parcell or Tract of
Land Containing that piece where formerly the old
Vander Doncks House stood together w'th ye

APPENDIX.

Meadow Ground & Planting ffield ye North side of w'ch said ffield by ye marked Trees is their North Bounds soe to run West to Hudsons River & East to Bronx his River w'th all ye Vpland from Broncks his River afores'd Southward to West Chest'r old Path & soe West to ye Meadow Ground w'ch cometh from ye Wadeing Place w'th all ye Meadow from ye Stake to ye Eastward of ye said Wadeing Place & soe along as Harlem River Runns into Hudsons River Reserving Thirty Acres of Meadow Ground only out of ye said proporcon of Land unto John Archer according to agreem't made between him & ye said Elias Doughty as in the Bill of Sale aforementconed is sett forth of w'ch said parcell or Tract of Land & pr'misses or ye greatest part thereof they ye said Wm. Betts & George Tippett or their Assignes are now in *actuall* & reall possession; Now Know Yee That by vertue of ye Commission & Authority unto mee given by his Royall Highness I have Ratifyed Confirmed & Graunted & by these pr'sents doe Ratify Confirme & Graunt unto ye aforenamed Wm. Betts & George Tippett their Heyres & Assignes ye aforementconed Parcell & Tract of Land Together w'th all ye Meadowes Wood Land, Pastures, Marshes, Waters, Creeks, & all other Proffitts Comoditves, & Emolum'ts to ye said Parcell or Tract of Land & Premisses within ye Bounds & Lymitts afores'd described belonging or in any wise appertaining w'th all other particulars & Benefitts in any Clause of their Bill of Sale made mention off w'th this Provisoe that what is herein Graunted doe noe way pr'judice ye New Towne of ffordham nor what hath been done by my Ord'r towards their

Settlem't To have & to hold all & Singular ye s'd Parcell & Tract of Land & Premisses w'th them & every of their Appertenances to ye said Wm. Betts & George Tippett their Heyres & Assigne unto ye proper use & Behoofe of ye said Wm. Betts & George Tippett their Heyres & Assignes forever Rendring & Paying such Dutyes & Acknowledgm'ts As now are or hereafter shall bee Constituted & Establisht by ye Lawes of this Governm't under ye Obedience of his Royall Highness his Heyres & Successors. Given under my Hand & Sealed w'th ye Seale of ye Province at fforte James in New Yorke this 20th day of ffebr'ry. in yo 23th Yeare of the Reigne of o'r Soveraigne Lord the King &c. Annoq Dm 1670.

I do hereby Certify the aforegoing to be a true Copy of the Original Record Compared therewith By Me. LEWIS A. SCOTT, *Secretary.*

INDEX.

Aarsen, Jan. 7.
Ackerman, William G. 53, 56.
Albany Post Road, 7, 11, 16, 18, 30, 32, 33, 45.
Allaire, Anthony, 21.
Allen, Jacamiah, 23.
Amusettes, 32.
Andros, Gov'r, 15.
Appleton, Wm. H. 47, 56.
Aqueducts, 62.
Archer, John (Jan Arcer), 7, 8, 15, 49, 66, 67, 73.
Archer, Matthias, Anthony, Benjamin, 22.
Armand, Col. 33.
Arnold, Gen. Benedict, 19.
Arnold, Dr. E. S. F. 60.
Arsdan, Benjamin, 22.
Aston, Abraham, 21.
Atherton, H. L. 56.

Babcock, Charles H. P. 49.
Babcock, Samuel D. 47, 56.
Bailey, Nathaniel P. 31.
Bainbridge, Rev. Thos. 45.
Bangs, Rev. I. D. 45.
Barch, Rev. Thomas, 45.
Barkins, Daniel, 49.
Barney, Hiram, 55.

INDEX.

Barnstable, 9.
Barracks, 27.
Barrett, Hannah, 10.
Barrett, John, 10, 42.
Barrett, Samuel, 10.
Barrier Gate, 17, 32.
Bastine, Stephen, 22.
Bates, Martin, 47, 56.
Battalion, The South, 21.
Battery, King's, 31.
Battery, The, 23.
Beekman, 20.
Bend, George H. 56.
Berrien, Abraham, 53.
Berrien, George, 21.
Berrien, Samuel, 53.
Berrien, Rev. William, 53.
Berrien's Neck, 10.
Bettner, J. E. 56.
Betts, Alice, 9.
Betts, Hopestill, 9.
Betts, John, 9.
Betts, Joseph, 44.
Betts, Mehitable, 10.
Betts, Samuel, 9.
Betts, William, 9, 11, 14, 21, 22, 68, 70, 71, 73.
Block House, 14.
"Blue Bell" Fort, 25.
Boar Hill, 32.
Bolton, Rev. Cornelius W. 46.
Boston, 16.
Boston Post Road, 16, 18, 19, 20, 30.
Bowling Green, 22.

Boynton, Rev. George M. 47.
Brann, Rev. Henry A. 48, 49.
Bridges, 14, 15, 17, 18, 28, 29, 32, 33, 35.
Broad Street, 20.
Broadway, 5.
Bronck, Jonas, 2.
Bronck's Land, 2, 13.
Bronx, Broncks, Bronckes, Bronckx his, Bronex
    River, 1, 2, 5, 8, 9, 14, 31, 63.
Bronx Heights, 28.
Brown, Rev. A. B. 45.
Brown, E. F. 56.
Brown, Ezekial, Henry, 22.
Brown, Fred'k, Gilbert, Robert, 21.
Brown, Rev. O. E. 45.
Brown, Rev. Paul R. 45.
Brown, Rev. T. James, 46.
Browne, Hendrick, Jr., 21.
Browning, Rev. Wm. F. 45.
Bryant, Capt. 34, 36.
Buckout, Matthias, 16.
Burr, Aaron, 18.
Burr, Rev. Charles H. 47.
Bursen, Henry, 21.
Bussing, John, 61.
Bussing's Point, 51.

CANADA, 17.
Cannon, 20, 23.
Cammann Place, 31.
Carpenter, Newton, 47.
Carter, Rev. A. B. 46.
"Causey" (Causeway), The, 14.

INDEX.

Central Avenue, 61.
"Charles," The, 12.
Charleston, S. C. 18.
Chasseurs, 32, 39.
Chevaux-de-frise, 25.
Christ Church, Riverdale, 47.
Church du St. Esprit, 18.
Church of the Mediator, 46.
City Island, 17.
Claflin, H. B. 31.
Clevinger, George, 11.
Clinton, Gen. 25, 26.
Coast Survey, 29.
Cock Hill, 13, 25.
Cock (Cox), John, 21, 22, 23.
Cock's (Cox) Tavern, 23.
Cole, James, 45.
Colendonck, 5.
Colgate, Robert, 46, 56.
Colonie of Nepperhaem, 5, 42.
Columbia College, 19, 52.
Commissioners of Forfeiture, 49, 55, 56, 57.
Committee of Safety, 22, 23, 26.
Concklin, John, 10.
Concklin, Mehitable, 10.
Congress, Continental, 20, 22.
Congress, Provincial, 20, 22, 24, 26.
Connecticut, 7, 9.
Coons, Rev. Aaron, 47.
"Cooperstown," 55.
Corsa, Andrew, 51.
Corsa's Orchard, 26.
Corton, James, 43.

INDEX.

Cortwright, John, Edward, 21.
"Cowboys," 33.
Cox, David B. 46, 53, 54.
Crawford, George, James, 21, 22.
Crawford, William, 43.
Cregier, John, 21.
Cregier, Capt. Thomas, 24.
Croft, Rev. H. 46.
Crook, Joseph, 49.
Cuthbert, B. 60.

DAVIES, REV. JOHN, 45.
Davis, Rev. A. B. 45.
Deen, Daniel, 21, 43.
Delafield Estate, 3.
Delafield, Joseph, 55.
Delafield, Lewis L. 55.
Delafield, Maturin L. 55.
De Lancey, Col. James, 32, 33, 41.
De Lancey, John, 51.
De Lancey, Thomas J. 46.
De Lancey's Mills, 36.
Delavall, Thomas, 11, 65.
De Rochambeau, 41.
Devoe, Daniel, 39, 40.
Devoe, Frederick, 39.
Devoe, John, 21.
Devoe, Moses, 44.
Devoe's Farm, 38.
Devoe's Point, 51.
De Vries, 4.
De Vries, Margaret, 12.
De Vries, Peter Rudolphus, 12.

INDEX.

Dickenson, Rev. Leigh Richmond, 46.
Dobb's Ferry, 36.
Dodd, Rev. Ira S. 47.
Dodge, Mary C. ("Sister Maria"), 58.
Dodge, Samuel N. 46.
Dodge, William E. 47, 55.
Dodge, William E., Jr. 47.
Donop Regiment, 32.
Doughty, Elias, 7, 8, 9, 11, 49, 65, 66, 70, 71.
Doughty, Rev. Francis, 6.
Douglas, Col. 31.
Dragoons, 39.
Duke of York, 63, 67.
Duke, William S. 56.
Dutch Ref'd Church, 8, 44.
Dyckman, Jacob, 17, 44.
Dyckman's Cut, 3.

EAGLETON, J. JOSEPH, 46.
East Chester, 14, 16, 33, 42, 44.
Eden, Joseph, 49.
Eden, Medcef, 49.
Edge Hill Chapel, 48.
Edsall, Thomas H. 54.
Ellison, Frances, 18.
Ellison, Robert, 18.
Ely, Col. 31.
Emmerick, Col. 32, 33, 38, 39, 40.
Emmons, Abraham, 21.
Emmons, Thomas, 21.
Erb Prinz Regiment, 32.
Esopus, 12.
Evans, Rev. Thomas, 45.

Ewen, Daniel, 51.
Ewen, Gen. John, 55.

FARRINGTON, BENJ., THOS., ROBT. 21.
"Ferry," The, 12, 13, 14.
Ferryman's Rates, 13.
Fire Engine House, 55.
Fire Ships, 25.
Fisher, Edward, 65.
Fisher, Samuel W. 45.
Fletcher, Gov'r, 15.
Flushing, 10.
Flypsen (Phillipse), Catherine, 12.
Flypsen (Phillipse), Margaret, 12.
Flypsen (Phillipse), Frederick, 11, 12, 15, 16.
"Font Hill," 60.
Fordham Dutch Church, 18.
Fordham Heights, 41.
Fordham Landing, 44.
Fordham, Manor of, 1, 44.
Fordham, Village of, 7, 8, 9, 11, 14, 15.
Forrest, Edwin, 57, 59.
Forster, George H. 56.
Fort, "Blue Bell," 25.
Fort, Cock Hill, 25.
Fort Independence, 19, 21, 26, 28, 29, 30, 31, 33, 34, 35, 36, 37, 38, 53.
Fort, The "King's Battery," 31.
Fort Lee, 25.
Fort, The "Negro," 31, 33, 36.
Fort "Number One," 29.
Fort "Number Two," 29.
Fort "Number Three," 21, 30.

INDEX.

Fort "Number Four," 21, 30.
Fort "Number Five," 30.
Fort "Number Six," 31.
Fort "Number Seven," 31.
Fort "Number Eight," 31.
Fort on Bussing Farm, 31, 36.
Fort Orange, 4.
Fort Prince Charles, 21, 30, 35.
Fort Swartwout, 26, 29.
Fort Washington, 2, 22, 25, 28, 29, 38.
Foster, C. W. 56.
Fountain, Usial, 21.
Fowler, Benjamin, 43.
Fowler, John, 23.
Fowler, Jonathan, 22.
Franklin, R. L. 56.
Free Bridge, The, 17, 18, 28, 29, 32, 33, 35.
French, Annetje, 12.
French Boarding School, 18.
French, Philip, 12.
Fry, Rev. William, 48.
Fuller, Joseph W. 53.

GAGE, LADY, 23.
Gallahue, Rev. A. C. 46.
Geer, William H. 53.
"General Putnam," Schooner, 24.
George III., Statue of, 22.
George's Point, 16.
German Regiments, 32.
Gibson, Edwin P. 46.
Giles, Wm. Ogden, 19, 30, 46, 53.
Gist, Col. 38, 40.

INDEX.

Godwin, Joseph H. 46, 52.
Goodridge, Frederick, 2, 47, 56.
Graham, Col. 26.
Grammar School, 62.
Green, Isaac, 21, 22.
Green, Rev. John C. 45.
Green, William, 21, 22.
Greene, Gen. 28.
Guereneau, John, 22.
Gun Hill, 62.

HADDEN (HADON, HEDDY, HEDGER), JOHN, 11, 14, 42, 69, 70, 73.
Hadley, George, 22, 53, 56.
Hadley, Isaac, 21.
Hadley, Joseph, 10, 16, 21, 42.
Hadley, Mehitable, 10.
Hadley, William, 21, 22, 43, 44, 55.
"Half Moon," The, 13.
Halsey, Daniel, 49.
Halsey's Tavern, 49.
Hardenbrook, Margaret, 12.
Harlem, 10, 13.
Harlem River, 1, 25.
Harriman, Laura, 56.
Haskin, John B. 31.
Hatfield, Rev. Henry, 45.
Hayden, James A. 55.
Heath, Gen. 25, 26, 31, 33, 34, 36, 37.
Hebard, Rev. E. 45.
Heights, 1, 9, 40, 41.
Hessians, 28, 32.
High Bridge, 8.

Hills, 2, 7, 10, 13, 21, 25, 26, 29, 32.
Hitchcock, Mehitable, 10.
Hitchcock, Samuel, 10.
Holden, John, 69, 71.
Holland, 5, 12.
Hollister, Thompson N. 47.
Holt, George C. 54.
Honeywell, Israel, 45.
Howe, Gen. 27, 31.
Hoyt, Rev. Philip L., 45.
Hudson, Henry, 3.
Hudson Park, 9.
Hudson River, 1, 2, 5, 8, 9, 29.
Hughes, Archbishop, 57.
Hughes, Mother Angela, 57.
Humphreys, Rev. Humphrey, 45.
Hunt, David, 43.
Husted's Heights, 40, 41.
Hutchins, Waldo, 32, 55.
Hyatt's Tavern, 20, 21, 35.

INDIAN CASTLE, 3.
"Indian Fields," The, 41.
Iron Foundry, 54.
Irving, Washington, 13.
Island, 2, 3.

JAMES, D. WILLIS, 56.
Janes, Bishop, 48.
Jerome, Mother, 58.
Johnson, Elias, 53, 54.
Johnson, Gilbert, 54.
Johnson, Isaac G. 46, 47, 48, 54.

Jones, William, 42.
"Jonker," 1.

Kellogg, David B. 47.
Kelly, Rev. R. H. 45, 48.
Kern, Rev. J. O. 48.
Koskeskick, 4.
Keyes, Rev. Charles C. 45.
Kieft, 4.
"King's Battery," 31.
King's Bridge, The, 14, 15, 17, 18.
King's Bridge Hotel, 17.
King's Bridge Marble, 3.
King's Ferry, 28.
King Philip's War, 14.
Knight, Madame, 16.
Knowlton, George W. 47.
Knyphausen, Gen. 28, 29.
Knyphausen Regiment, 32.
"Koop-al," Jan. 7.

"Labadists," The, 12.
Lake, 2.
Langdon, Jervis, 53.
Langdon Rolling Mill Co. 53.
Lasher, Col. 28.
Lausanne, University of, 18.
Lawrence, John C. 45.
Lawrence, Samuel, 22, 24.
Laws, Rev. Gustav, 48.
Leib Regiment, 32.
Lent, Abraham, Jr. 49.
Lent, Rev. Isaac H. 48.

Lewis, Thomas, 11, 65.
Lexington, 20.
Leyden, 4.
Lime Kilns, 3.
Lincoln, Gen. 33, 34, 36, 38.
Livingston, Janet, 19.
Llonart, 56.
Long Island, 26.
Lord, Rev. William R. 47.
Losberg Regiment, 32.
Lothrop, Rev. Mr. 9.
Lounsbery, Henry R. 54.
Lounsbery, William, 23.
Lovelace, Gov. Francis, 9, 11.
"Lovers' Lane," 39.
Lovett, Rev. Noble, 45.
"Lower Cortlandts," 32.
"Lower Mills," 44.
Lowther, Rev. S. 48.

McCormick, Rev. D. 48.
Maccakassin, Macackcsin, 7, 63.
Macomb, Alexander, 49.
Macomb, Mary C. P. 52.
Macomb, Robert, 51, 52.
Macomb, Gen. 52.
Macomb's Mill, 51, 52.
Macomb's Mountains (Adirondacks), 51.
Macomb Street, 14.
Macomb's Dam, 51.
"Maine," The, 13, 15.
Mali, H. W. T. 31.
Mamaroneck, 23.

INDEX.

Manetto, 4.
Manhattan Island, 2, 3, 6, 10, 13, 28, 29.
Manor of Fordham, 1, 8.
Manor of Phillipsburgh, 12, 42, 43, 49, 55, 56.
Marshall, John, 69, 71.
Martin, Monsieur, 26.
Maryland, 11.
Merrill, Thomas, 21.
Merson, L. O. 48.
Methodist Church, 44.
Micena, Rev. Fr. 48.
Mifflin, Gen. 24.
Mile Square, 11, 43.
Mile Square Road, 32, 38, 43, 60, 62.
Mill Creek, 2.
Mills, 5, 32, 51, 52.
Mirback Regiment, 32.
Moller, George, 53.
Montgomery, Gen. Richard, 19, 20, 30.
Montressor, Col. 23, 37.
Montressor's (Randall's) Island, 37.
Moore, Jacob, 22.
Moore's Tavern, 22.
Morris, Augustus F. 54.
Morrisania, 2, 37.
Morrison, David M. 54.
Mosholu, 2, 9, 31, 44, 45, 54, 60, 62.
Mott, John, 46, 47.
Mount St. Vincent, 1, 12, 25, 56.
Munro, James, 21.
Muscoote, 6.
Muskota, 7.
Myers, T. Bailey, 46.

INDEX.

Neperan, 7.
Nepperhaem Colonie, 5.
Nepperhaem River, 4, 63.
Nepperhaem Tract, 5.
New Amsterdam, 5, 6, 12.
New Castle, 36.
New Jersey, Palisades of, 2.
New Rochelle, 28, 33.
New York, 1, 2, 7, 15.
New York City & Northern R. R. 60.
New York "Gazetteer," The, 19.
New York & Harlem R. R. 61.
New York Hydraulic M'f'g & Bridge Co. 52.
Nicholas, Col. 26.
Nicholls, Perkins, 3, 52.
Nicoll, Sec'y Matthias, 8, 49, 75.
Nicoll, Gov'r Richard, 6, 8, 63, 65, 67.
Nieuwhoff, 7.
Nieuw Netherland, 6.
Nimham, 39, 41.
Nixon, Rev. Cyrus, 46.
Nodine, Andrew, 43.
Norris, Henry, 22.
Norris, Jordan, 22.

Oakley, David, 43.
Oakley, David, Jr. 22.
Oakley, Joseph, Jr. 21.
Oakley, Moses, 22.
Oakley, Thomas, 21.
Odell, Abraham, 21.
Odell, Isaac, 43.
Odell, John, 21.

Okeley, Thomas, 67.
Oksanne, John, 65.
Olaff Park, 9, 61.
Oldrin, Rev. E. 45.
O'Neale, Hugh, 6, 7, 63, 65.
O'Neale, Mrs. Hugh, 6, 7, 11, 63, 65.
O'Neale Patent, 7, 8, 11.
O'Neill, Rev. Fr. 48.
Oost-Dorp, 7, 9.
Orange, Fort, 4.
Ostrander, Rev. A. 46.
Opdyke, George, 60.
Oudinot, E. S. 48.

Packamiens, 4.
Palisades of New Jersey, 2.
Palmer, Benjamin, 17.
Paparinamin,
Papirinimin, } 7, 9, 12, 13, 14, 17, 28, 49, 51, 63.
Pappereneman,
Parker, James, 21.
Park, The Riverdale, 56.
Parsons, Gen. 34.
Parsons, M.D. John, 53.
Patents, 7, 8, 11.
Paulding, Col. 26.
Paulus Hook, 26.
Peck, Rev. E. M. 47.
Perry, Rev. Salmon C. 45.
Petrie, George H. 54.
Phiilipsburgh, 1.
Phillipsburgh Manor, 12, 60.
Phillipse, Adolphus, 12.

INDEX.

Phillipse, Annetje, 12.
Phillipse (Flypsen), Catherine, 12.
Phillipse, Eva, 12.
Phillipse, Col. Frederick, 16, 17, 19, 49, 57.
Phillipse (Flypsen), Frederick, 11, 12, 65.
Phillipse 2d, Frederick, 12, 15.
Phillipse (Flypsen), Margaret, 12.
Phillipse's Mills, 32.
"Phœnix," The, 25.
Plantation, The Yonkers, 1.
"Planting Field," Vander Donck's, 5, 9.
Plested, Rev. Wm. 46.
Poe, Edgar Allan, 52.
Point, 3.
Pontoon Bridge, 30.
Post, Abraham, 21, 24.
Post, Dennis, 21, 24.
Post, Hendrick, 43.
Post, Isaac, 21, 24.
Post, Israel, 21, 24.
Post, Jacob, 21, 24.
Post, Lewis, 21, 24.
Post, Martin, 21, 24.
Post, William, 21, 24.
Post Riders, 17.
Post Roads, 7, 11, 16, 18, 19, 20, 30, 32, 33, 45.
Potter, Rt. Rev. Horatio, 46.
Powder Magazine, The old, 18.
Prince, William Henry, 41.
Prinz Carl Regiment, 32.
Pusher, Henry, 21.
Putnam, Albert E. 54.
Pyne, Moses Taylor, 56.

INDEX.

Pyne, Percy R. 47.

QUEBEC, 19.
Queen's Rangers, 39.
Quimby, 8.

RAMSEY, JOHN, 49.
Randolph, Edmund D. 60.
Ranelagh, Sarah, Viscountess, 19.
Rangers, 32.
Rawdon, Lord, 32.
Rechgawac, 4.
Regiments, 32.
Regina, Mother, 58.
Rennselaerswyck, 4.
Renwick, Prof. James, 52.
Revolutionary War, 18, 19.
Rhinebeck, 19.
Rich, Abraham, 22.
Rich, James, 22.
Rich, Thomas, 22, 42.
Rickman, Tobias, 21.
Rider, Robert, 72.
Ridge, 2, 3.
Riker, James, 13.
Riverdale, 2, 12.
Riverdale Institute, 62.
Riverdale Presbyterian Church, 66.
Riverdale Road. 29.
Rogers, Col. 33.
"Rose," The, 24, 25.
Rose, William, 21.
Ross, Major, 40.

Ryer, Edward, 21.
Ryer, John, 21.
Ryder, Jacob, 42.
Ryder, John, 43.

SAGE, WARREN B. 29, 30, 47, 54.
Santhier's Map, 29.
Saw Kill, 4, 16.
Schermerhorn, A. 56.
Schools, 18.
Schuyler, Gen. 18.
Schwab, Gustav, 31.
Scituate, 9.
Scott, Gen. 33, 38.
Scott, Lewis A. 77.
Scrymser, James, 47.
Sealey, Benjamin T. 53.
Seaman, Rev. R. 45.
Sebring, 20.
Segur, Rev. Fred'k W. 45.
Sergeant, Joseph R. 54.
Sharpe, John, 66, 75.
Sherwood, Jeremiah, 43.
Sherwood, Thomas, 42, 43.
Shorack-Kappock, 3, 63.
Shrader, Rev. Dr. 48.
Shrive, Rev. J. G. 45.
Sidney, James C. 46.
Sietz Regiment, 32.
Silleck, Rev. John A. 45.
Simcoe, Lt. Col. 32, 39, 40.
Sisters of Charity, 56.
"Skinners," 33.

INDEX.

Smith, Edward, 42.
Smith, Rev. E. 45.
Smith, Francis, 21.
Smith, Henry M. 51.
Smith, Russell, 46.
Smith, William, 11.
Smith, Rev. W. H. 46.
"Sons of Liberty," 23.
Sorquapp, 7.
Spanish Bell, 56.
Spaulding, Henry F. 47, 56.
Spring Street, 30.
Spuyten Duyvil ("Spiting Devil"), 9, 13, 15.
Spuyten Duyvil Creek, 1, 2, 5, 25, 29.
Spuyten Duyvil Neck, 10, 29.
Spuyten Duyvil Point, 3, 53.
Spuyten Duyvil Ridge, 2, 3, 30, 35.
Spuyten Duyvil & Port Morris R. R. 61.
St. Elizabeth's Church, 49.
St. John's Benevolent Society, 48.
St. John's Church, 44, 48.
St. Patrick's Temperance Society, 48.
St. Vincent's Free School, 60.
Stage Coach, 17.
States General, 5.
Stebbins, Rev. Henry H. 47.
Steenwyck, Cornelis, 8.
Stevenson, Edward, 43.
Stewart, Col. 40.
Stockbridge Indians, 38, 39.
Stone, Henry L. 47, 56.
Strang, Peter O. 29.
Strang, Mrs. 54.

INDEX.

Streets, 5, 14, 20, 30.
Stuyvesant, Peter, 5, 6, 9, 12.
Swartwout, Col. 26.

TARLETON, LT. COL. 39, 40, 41.
Tarleton, Rev. W. 46.
Tarrytown, 33.
Tasker, Rev. David, 47.
Taverns, 17, 20, 21, 22, 23, 32, 35, 49.
Taylor, Charles, 21.
Taylor, Elnathan, Jr. 21.
Taylor, Elijah, 21.
Taylor, Henry, 21.
Taylor, Jacob, 21.
Taylor, Joseph, 42.
Taylor, Moses, 42, 43.
Ten Broeck, Gen. 38.
Tequemet, 4.
Tetard, Rev. John Peter, 18, 62.
Tetard's Farm, 19, 31, 33.
Tetard's Hill, 7, 21, 28, 29, 30, 32, 41, 62.
Thomas, Col. 26.
Thompson, Wm. W. 47.
Thomson, Samuel, 54, 55.
Thorn's Dock, 9.
Throg's Neck, 27.
Tier, Daniel, 61.
Tippett, Dorcas, 10, 53.
Tippett, George, 2, 9, 10, 11, 14, 42, 49, 53, 67, 70, 71, 73.
Tippett 2d, George, 16.
Tippett, Henry, 10.
Tippett, James, 53.

Tippett, Martha, 33.
Tippett, Mehitable, 10.
Tippett, Thomas, 22, 53.
Tippett, William, 53.
Tippett's ("Tibbitt's") Brook, 2, 10, 16, 10, 51, 52
Tippett's Hill, 10, 21, 25, 26, 29, 32, 36, 41.
Tremper, George R. 60.
Trimback Regiment, 32.
Trinity Parish, 53.
Tolls, 13, 15, 18.
Totten, Col. 52.
Townsend, Lord, 23.

UNDERHILL, IZARELL, 21.
"Upper Cortlandts," 32, 55.

VALENTINE, ABRAHAM, 46.
Valentine, Daniel, 46.
Valentine, Gilbert, 60.
Valentine, Isaac, 23, 33, 36, 51.
Valentine, John, 51.
Valentine, Matthias, 42, 51.
Valentine, William, 61.
Valentine's Hill, 32, 41, 62.
Valentine's House, 33, 36.
Valentine's Ridge, 2.
Van Cortlandt, Augustus, 23, 41, 46, 51, 54, 60.
Van Cortlandt, Catherine, 12.
Van Cortlandt Estate, 5, 11, 16, 61.
Van Cortlandt, Eva, 12.
Van Cortlandt, Frederick, 20, 21, 32, 51.
Van Cortlandt, Jacobus, 1, 5, 15.
Van Cortlandt, Col. James, 20, 21, 23, 32, 33, 43, 55
Van Cortlandt Lake, 2.

Van Cortlandt Mansion, 14, 41.
Van Cortlandt's Ridge, 1.
"Van Cortlandt's," 9, 60.
Van Cortlandt's Mills, 5.
"Van Cortlandt's" Woods, 39, 40, 41.
Van Courtlandt Vault, 23.
Vander Donck, Dr. Adraien ("Vander Duncke"), 1, 4. 8, 51, 60, 63.
Vander Donck, Cornelis, 6.
Vander Donck's Bowerie, 6, 9.
Vander Donck's House, 5, 75.
Vander Donck's "Planting Field," 5, 9, 11, 61.
Van Gaasbeck, Rev. D. W. C. 48.
Van Tassell, Caleb, 45.
Varian, Jacob, 45.
Varian Jacob H. 45.
Varian, William A., M.D. 53.
Vault Hill, 2, 5, 23.
Vermilye, Abrm. 21, 61.
Vermilye, Fred'k, 21, 61.
Vermilye, Isaac, 44, 51.
Vermilye, Joshua, 21, 61.
Vermilye, Petrus, 18.
Vermilye, Thomas, 17.
Verveelen, Daniel, 14.
Verveelen, Johannes, 13, 14, 49.
Vincent, Charles, 42.
Virginia, 31.
Vitrey, Lewis, 10, 49.
Vitrey, Mehitable, 10, 49.
Von Hanger, Capt. 32.
Von Pfister, Alexander, 49.
Von Wurmb, Lt. Col. 32, 33.

INDEX.

"Wading Place." The, 4, 13.
Waldeckers, 28.
Warner, Charles, 43, 53.
Warner, John, 21, 22, 24, 43, 44, 56.
Warner, William, 21, 22, 24, 43, 44, 56.
Warner's Store, 45, 62.
Ward, The 23d, 2.
Washington, Fort, 2.
Washington, Gen. George, 24, 27, 31, 35, 41
Watch House, 32.
Weckquaeskeek, 3.
Weeks, Edward, 43.
Wertz, George, 22.
Westchester, 7, 9, 10, 11.
Westchester County, 12.
Westchester Path, 7, 16.
West Farms, 1, 2.
West India Company, 5, 12.
Wetmore, William C. 54.
Wheatly, Rev. Richard, 45.
White Plains, 1, 19, 28, 31.
Whiting Estate, 3.
Whiting, James R. 46, 54, 55.
Wickerscreek Indians, 3.
Wiessenback Regiment, 32.
Wildes, Rev. George D. 47.
Willard, E. K. 48, 60.
Williams Bridge, 31, 36.
Williams' House, 23, 33, 37.
Williams, Samuel, 22.
Wilson, Rev. William T. 46, 53.
"Wine Cellar," Dominic Tetard's, 18.
Woelwarth Regiment, 32.

INDEX.

Wood, Abraham, 45.
Woodlawn Cemetery, 9, 61.
Woodlawn Heights, 2, 9, 12, 38, 39, 60.
Woodlawn Methodist Church, 48.
Woodworth, W. W. 56, 61.
Wooster, Gen. 34, 38.
Wright, Orderly, 41.
Wright, Rev. Daniel I. 45.

Yonkers,
Younckers, } 1, 2, 4, 9, 10, 12, 14, 19, etc.
Younkers,
Yonkers Episcopal Society, 44.
Yonkers Plantation, The, 1, 16.
Yonkers Precinct, 42.
Yonkers River, 2, 52.
Yorkshire, North Riding of, 42.

www.ingramcontent.com/pod-product-compliance
Lightning Source LLC
Chambersburg PA
CBHW030409170426
43202CB00010B/1546